American Mother

Also by Colum McCann

FICTION
Apeirogon
Thirteen Ways of Looking
TransAtlantic
Let the Great World Spin
Zoli
Dancer
Everything in This Country Must
This Side of Brightness
Songdogs
Fishing the Sloe-Black River

NON-FICTION
Letters to a Young Writer
The Book of Men (Editor)

PLAYS
Yes! (with Aedin Moloney)

AMER ICAN MOTHER

Colum McCann
with Diane Foley

Etruscan Press

Etruscan Press
Wilkes University
84 West South Street
Wilkes-Barre, PA 18766
(570) 408-4546

Wilkes
University

www.etruscanpress.org

Published 2024 by Etruscan Press
Printed in the United States of America
Cover photo: Jonathan Wiggs/*The Boston Globe* via Getty Images
Cover and interior design and typesetting by Lisa Reynolds
The text of this book is set in Hoefler Text.

First Edition

17 18 19 20 5 4 3 2 1

Library of Congress Cataloguing-in-Publication Data
Library of Congress Control Number: 2023937629

Please turn to the back of this book for a list of the sustaining
funders of Etruscan Press.

This book is printed on recycled, acid-free paper.

To live in the hearts we leave behind is not to die.

Thomas Campbell

This book is dedicated to
Kayla, Peter, Steven and Jim.
Also to Rita.

And to mothers everywhere.

BOOK ONE

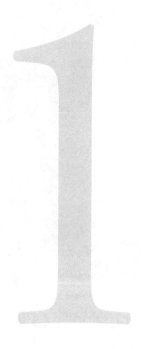

1

October 2021
Alexandria, Virginia

She wakes in the hotel dark. A scattering of streetlights through the thin curtains. There, in the distance, Washington D.C. – city of truths, half-truths, double-truths, lies. One sure truth: her son is seven years gone now, and this morning she will sit with one of his killers.

The prospect ties a knot of nerves at the base of her neck. It is not simply that she has no idea what to expect from him: it is just as much that she has little idea what to expect from herself. A symphony of confusion. Compassion. Revenge. Bitterness. Mercy. Loss. Grace.

Throughout the night she has prayed even more than usual. Beseeched the highest powers. Scoured the darkness and the brightness too. Spent hours wondering what to call him. *Alexanda. Alexe. Alex. Kotey. Mister Kotey.* No. Not *mister.* Not that. She is, after all, at 73 years, almost twice his age.

But there is protocol too. Decency. Everyone deserves a name, even those who want to take away the names of others.

She clicks on the light. The hotel room is spacious and sparsely furnished. She slides open the closet door. Inside, hanging neatly, are the clothes she has chosen. Her long, patterned dress. A gray turtleneck to go underneath. A stylish Libyan shawl given to her by Jim many years ago, after his first capture. The high shoes that are neither sensible nor comfortable. On the bathroom counter she has laid out the gold hoop earrings and a gold Ecuadorian necklace to place at her throat: a medal of the Blessed Mother. A Croatian bracelet representing the decades of the Rosary. Gifts from her mother.

Her make-up is light. She uses a small stretch of lipstick. Her dark hair is one of her last vanities: she combs it with hand and brush, fanning it sideways over and over again.

She consults the mirror. Her look is layered. Confident, even elegant, but beneath it she is raw, tight, vulnerable. How to proceed? How to dignify this stung heart? How to tamp down the grief? How to look him in the eye? How to bypass the hatred? How to use the machinery of her wits?

She returns to the bedside where she kneels once more. *Lord, make me an instrument of your peace. Make me merciful. Give me strength.*

The courthouse room is large. Windowless. The light is fluorescent. The tables are arranged in a rectangle. Kotey sits alone near the front of the room, head bowed. He is in his late-30s, broad-shouldered, his hair shorn close. A bristly beard of medium length. He wears a green short-sleeved jumpsuit. His feet are shackled, but not his hands which are clasped in front of him. Even sitting down, he is tall, and appears strong— much stronger than she expected.

She approaches with sure steps. The chairs have been arranged so that she will sit opposite him. No glass protectors. No barriers. Just a conference room table. There is enough social distance that she doesn't have to worry about reaching across to shake his hand. The thought had worried her earlier: she did not want to have to touch him. She removes her Covid mask: everyone in the room has been vaccinated. Kotey remains seated, his head still slightly bowed, his hands roiling over each other. His fingernails, she notices, are long and clean.

There are seven others in the room to monitor the conversation. Three from the defense. Three from the prosecution. A family friend alongside her to help her ask questions. But essentially it is only her and him.

"Good morning, Alexanda," she says as she approaches.

She appears cheerful, always cheerful, even at the most difficult of times. It is one of her natural disguises. She is known for her smile, her grace, her ease of movement.

She bears down hard on the middle of the name and stretches the syllables out on elastic. "Alex-aahn-da." Her accent is pure New England. She did not want to call him *Alexe*, his preferred name and the one the defense has used since he was brought to America four months ago. Nor did she want to abbreviate it to *Alex*, the name the prosecutors have called him in interrogations.

Alexanda. The same name that his own mother had given him. He should be allowed at least that. There is a dignity in that.

His eyes lift slightly and he gives the tiniest nod. His are complicated eyes, deep brown, baggy with darkness, and it is difficult to tell what they contain.

"Good morning," he says.

She scoots up the hardback chair once more, settles her shawl around her. She wants him to immediately know that she is not afraid of him, not one bit. She places her hands on the table: her bracelet jangles. He shifts his feet, and the titanium shackles make their own slight sound. Bracelets and shackles.

She will not cry. The last time she cried was the day Jim died. Seven years ago. She smiles instead: steely yet warm. She is a woman of resolve. Her great accomplishment is the containment of her sorrow within.

"You can call me Diane."

He nods and slides his fingers over the back of his hand: as if the hands are open and closed at the same time. It strikes her that he is a dark doorway: somewhere there, in front of her, her son waits.

He has already pleaded guilty to eight counts, including conspiracy to the murder of James Foley, Steven Sotloff, Peter Kassig and Kayla Mueller. Each of the counts will lead to a mandatory life sentence. The meeting now is part of an extraordinary plea agreement: he is in a Virginia jail, and he has agreed to speak with the families of the victims if they want, before sentencing. She is the first of the victims to say that she would meet him, and perhaps, in the end, she will be the only one.

But even among her own family and friends there is doubt, anger, frustration, grief. Why give Kotey any platform? Why give him any dignity at all? Hasn't he already confessed? Why not let him rot in a cell? Why open yourself to a terrorist? Why give him time? Even a modicum of respect? Don't we know him already? The black hood. The eyes. The desert sands. The orange jumpsuit. The kneeling figure. The slice of the knife across the neck. The head, then, placed grotesquely upon her son's back. Why open the agonies of the past?

Others have said that it is courageous of her to meet with him, that she is doing something extraordinary. But it isn't bravery, she doesn't think of it as that, no, not at all. Nor is it an act of grace or forgiveness. No. Perhaps it is just a refusal to be scared. Perhaps it is a way to say that you have not really killed my son. Perhaps it is as fundamental as that: *I am his mother and you have not killed him, and I am here to tell you that.*

"I hope," she says, "you're being treated well."

The room is electric with the unsaid. He half-nods.

"Your name," she says. "Alexanda. It means 'protector of the people.'"

She will discover later that his surname, Kotey, comes for Ghana, and that its African origin means "a kind soul."

Alexanda Kotey. Former British citizen. Former ISIS soldier and member of a group among them known in the newspapers as 'The Beatles.' Former drug dealer. Incarcerated now. Citizen of nowhere. A man who is bound now to spend his life in a small inescapable room.

He too smiles. It's a thin smile, but it disarms her, the early confidence of it. Still, she maintains her own, the unfailingly polite smile, the steely one, the warm one. It lasts through the silence as she arranges her notes in front of her.

She has been warned, over and over: *Be careful, Diane, this man is a liar.*

She saw him in court here, in Virginia, two months ago, from a distance. The death penalty had been withdrawn in negotiations between the U.K. and the U.S. governments, and by agreement of all the families of the victims. He had pleaded guilty to eight counts, including four counts of conspiracy to murder. He had shown no emotion then. Not a twitch of it. He had glanced in her and her husband John's direction, but there was nothing there. His was a rote admission. He was a frozen sea. Nothing moving. She has told friends that she isn't here now to forgive him or placate him. No—she is here for something else. She hasn't quite figured it out. It's a deep-down gut feeling. And anything might happen. He might stonewall her. He might try to taunt her with rhetoric and ridicule. He might even descend to the psychopathic: she has been told how dangerous he is. Still, she must engage. She simply must. Even against the advice of friends and family. She is here now. There is no going back. It was what Jim would have done, to rescue something from the barren. To know *who*. To know *why*. There was no doubt whatsoever that Jim would have been first in line to talk with him. But she is not sure she can uncover anything of worth at all. Maybe just her own raw wounds. Maybe that is all. Maybe she is making an enormous mistake. Perhaps those who stayed home in the northeast are correct: she should have remained where she was. There are so many people to look after. She is a wife, a mother, a grandmother, a daughter too. Her own mother, Olga, is 95 years old. Her grandson, Colin, is just a week old. And oh, there are no better gifts than a grandchild in the crook of your arm.

Still, she has committed herself to the moment. To know the *how* of a loved-one's death is to better know the loved-one's life. To more fully love the loved one. To keep that life alive.

The first few questions must set the tone. She wants to disarm him, unbalance him, travel beyond who he apparently shows himself to be.

"So, Alexanda," she says. "Do you have any questions for me?"

A small shiver circles the room.

"No," he says after a moment. "I'm just here for you. To answer yours."

His accent is pure London. Sharp. Direct. Not as Cockney as she had expected. It sounded already as if there was schooling within it, although she knew already that he had not gone anywhere beyond high school, that there were years on the streets of Shepherd's Bush, drug dealing, cocaine, fighting, gangs, before he converted to Islam and made his trip to doom.

He has had years to contemplate these answers: two in a prison in northern Syria, several months now in Virginia where he has been given a strong team of defenders and a full opportunity at trial. This, she knows, is the beauty of the American justice system. The system has not served her well in the past, she thinks. Nor did it serve Jim or the other dead hostages. But it is serving the people now, and she is grateful to the prosecutors who have allowed her this moment which lies, she knows, in the territory between doom and redemption.

"But my question is about your questions," she says. "What questions do you have of me?"

His eyes become unhooded for a moment. He glances up newly at her. If they were playing chess, she might have put out her bishop, and he is trying now to figure if his response should be a horse or a pawn.

"About James?" he says. "Can I call him James?"

"I call him Jim."

"I didn't know James very well."

Her Jim, his James. Her intimacy, his distance. Her bracelets, his shackles. Her present, his past.

Still, he appears different from the gaunt, haunted photos from his days in Syria. He has put on weight. He is muscled. And there is an almost-gentle edge to his speech, a politeness, or at very least, a control. He has most likely practiced this, with his attorneys perhaps, and a facilitator. He has figured out what it is that he has to say. It's a tricky situation: she has arrived with the prosecutors, and he has arrived with the defense. Outside the door, the FBI waits. It is not a legal proceeding, but there are certain things that have to be carefully said. The conversation belongs only to Diane and him, but they are aware that they are entering new territory: perhaps the real trial here is the human reckoning between them both.

Nothing is being recorded. All phones and audio devices are out of the room. But over the course of the next few hours every syllable is a whistle of truth and lies.

She listens: this is her job now, she must listen.

He is guilty, he admits, entirely guilty of the counts as they were presented to him—conspiracy to murder, hostage-taking resulting in death, and providing material support to the Islamic State. He will take his punishment. "I accept what has happened to me," he says. He has pleaded under western law, though he wishes he had been judged under the jurisprudence of Islam. The American system of justice is not one in which he believes. He pays it no respect. He has made his choices. "I had my superiors. I have done what was asked of me." He had been involved with the detention and treatment of hostages, yes. He had been told early on to "turn their skin blue." He physically beat James, yes, he admits it, but only twice over the two years of captivity—once a minor slap in the face through a prison grille when he thought James was insulting Islam, the second time with a series of blows alongside his fellow ISIS soldiers, including the late Mohammed Emwazi, known in the media as Jihadi John. It was a light beating for James, he suggests, "mostly body blows." He is not the person the press has made him out to be, he says, darting his eyes about the room. He was not present at the execution. He had not pulled the knife across her son's throat. He had not filmed the moment in the desert. He had not been there when her son's severed head was placed upon his back. He was a soldier of Islam, he says. "I was at war." He had responded to his superiors, but he did not murder any of the detainees. He felt impotent against orders, he says. He has killed people, yes. Once he shot a prisoner in the back of the head in cold blood. "I take responsibility for everything that I have done." He isn't shirking his past now, he says. "I made this choice, and you have the right to hear why." He knew what he was doing when he left Britain for Syria. He had crossed mountain ranges to get there. He had fought for many reasons, moral, political, religious. The U.S. invasion of Iraq. Guantanamo. Abu Ghraib. The treatment of Muslims worldwide. All his life he has pushed up against the imperial instinct. He had left behind his eight-year-old daughter. He hasn't yet concluded what regrets he has about his time in Syria, though he has some. He has questions, too, about the innocence of his victims, the morality of hostage-taking under the laws of the Islamic State, the language of the Sharia that was used during war. But ultimately, he says, he is guilty, yes, guilty, under U.S. law. He cannot deny it. Yet his guilt, he says, is technical. It is important that she knows it was done under the auspices of war. He was doing what he was told. "Everything I did," he says, "I did without malice."

She knows he is lying.

Minimal admission. Minimal remorse. Designed and tailored for just enough truth.

And yet there is something there—Diane can't tell what—hovering beneath the lies, another skin, another version of the truth, something visceral, something graspable, something to stretch towards.

She has heard from the prosecution and from former hostages that Emwazi was the most brutal of all, but that Kotey was not far behind. *Exceptionally cruel* was the language. The waterboarding. The starvation techniques. The chokeholds. The electric shocks. The psychological torture. The mock crucifixions. He claims that he only beat Jim twice, but the notion is doubtful, pathetic even, given all that she knows from the European hostages who managed to get home. They have said that Jim was treated the worst of all. He was subjected to continual harm, mental and physical. He was singled out for beatings.

This man here, she thinks. Not four feet away. He beat my son. He participated in the execution. Right here. In front of me. She can almost feel his breath drifting across the table.

He bows his head and murmurs as if towards the ground. "Emwazi had it in for James," he says, still staring down. It is a good trick that, she thinks: deflect the guilt, blame the dead. Mohammed Emwazi. Vaporized in a U.S. drone attack almost six years ago. A monster, yes. But a convenient monster now.

She hugs her arms tightly around herself. What use is all this? What good can come from asking Kotey further about these beatings? Why prolong the misery? What good will it serve to further uncover his cruelty? It is a matter of self-preservation for him. He will only continue to lie, and she does not want the time to dissolve into a cacophony of deceit. Besides, the conversation might slide a sharp blade under her own fingernails anyway, an echo torture of sorts.

One thing she knows for sure: she is not here for revenge.

The minutes slide by. Kotey retreats into the grand rhetoric of Islam, the complications of war, the tangled make-up of the state, Sharia law, lightning decisions, battlefield interpretations. He is good at it, the grandstanding, the misdirection, the bloviation. But there is something else there: she can't quite catch the pulse of it. What is it?

Why did he take the plea? Surely if he felt so strongly about his beliefs, he would have opted for a full trial?

Part of the plea agreement is that he can return to Britain after 15 years in American jails. Life without parole.

"Jail is jail," he says.

But if jail is jail, and if life is life, why not go to court and showcase his beliefs? If he really was peripheral to the executions—if he really is telling the truth—why not air that in public? He claims not to believe in the American system, but so far, the system seems to be treating him quite well: yes, he is in jail. But the death penalty has been taken away, and he is well-fed, protected, he has a team of defenders, he has had access to justice. It was, in fact, his own defense team who originally suggested that, if he pleaded guilty, he would talk with the victims and their families. As a way towards truth. As a path towards healing.

He appears so confident in his answers that she suspects for a moment that there might actually be a terrified man lying underneath. Or maybe it's nothing at all: maybe that's all it is, a shell of a soul, theatrically gifted—*that one may smile and smile and be a villain*—broken, psychotic, playing her like some strange human instrument.

She so desperately wants him to know what he took away from the world, what he stole: not just the journalist and activist James Wright Foley, her son, her oldest boy, but everything Jim represented down through the years. It is one of the reasons she has come here. To tell the truth. With no sentimentality. No schmaltz. Just the plain straightforward truth. "Jim was a teacher," she says to him, leaning forward, her bracelets rattling. He worked with juvenile delinquents. Unwed mothers too. As a journalist, he bore witness. Jim searched for the ground truth. He was fair, he was curious, he was even-tempered. He was interested in equanimity. Jim aspired to have moral courage. He was a man for others. When he became a journalist, he gave his life trying to expose the world to the suffering of the Syrian people. He was compelled to bear witness. He was a thoughtful son too. The older brother of five. A friend. He was widely loved. Jim saw the good in everyone. He believed in the complicated truth. He would have written Kotey's story—what is more, he would have gotten it entirely correct. She looks him in the eye. "He was a good person."

Kotey shifts his feet. The shackles sound out: not a high metallic sound, almost muted.

A mid-morning break is announced. She walks the long corridors of the Justice building. Messages on her phone. So many messages. John. Her daughter Katie. The Foley Foundation. She quickly scrolls through. "You are doing beautifully," says Jenn Donnarumma, a victim advocate from the prosecution team, but Diane is not sure at all, and she wonders if all of this is an extended mistake. And yet, then again, there is Jim. Always Jim, the spirit of Jim. He would have wanted to know. And there are other things to contemplate too. Perhaps Kotey will reveal the names of some of the higher-ups who have not yet been prosecuted? Perhaps he will give her a clue into the psychology of hostage-takers? Perhaps he will reveal the burial place of the bodies of Jim and the other dead hostages?

When she returns to the room, she is once again ready.

"What do you regret, Alexanda?"

"I haven't concluded yet what I regret," he says.

"What did you think of Jim?"

"I thought he was a typical white American."

"What else do you know of him?"

"I saw the documentary."

"Yes?"

"I thought he was an optimist, and I thought he was naïve, I don't mean this in a negative way, you understand?"

"He was a lot like you, Alexanda, don't you think?"

"I don't know."

"He was a truth seeker."

"Yes."

"He was dark-skinned like you."

No answer.

He glances up and says: "I have had a lot of time in isolation, a lot of time to think."

"I'm here to listen," she says.

He is at pains to tell her that he wants to escape from the cliché of being called a Beatle in the media, to move away from the sensationalism of the tabloids. It rankles him. "It's cheap and easy for the papers. I want people to view me in my reality." He thinks about his own mother, he says, and how she receives this sort of news. He has been labelled a thug, a soccer hooligan, but he's only ever been to two football matches, one when England played Yugoslavia when he was a child, and another when he went to a Leighton Orient game. The English Sunday newspapers said he supported a team named Queens Park Rangers, but he never did, it was just another way for the media to simplify him, stuff him in a pre-ordained box: there had been a blue-and-white QPR gnome outside his house belonging to his stepfather. This may sound to some like a small detail, but, he says, it is important to him. "The press wants to distort me, anything they can do to make a monster out of me." They are only interested in another easy cliché. Believe it or not, he says, he actually played baseball. American baseball, of all things. "First base in fact." Yes, he had been a drug dealer in his later teenage years, that is true. Cocaine. But there was more to it than that. He had been beaten by other London schoolboys at the age of 13. His radicalization had its roots in that thuggery. He converted from the Greek Orthodox faith. He found sanctuary in the mosque in Westbourne Park. He found, in Islam, the idea of a better, freer society. There were many layers of complication. His father was from Ghana but died when he was two years old. His mother, from Greece, is a therapist. He has an older brother in London who has long since disowned him. They can make him into a monster all they want, but he knows that there is a deeper truth.

Towards noon, Kotey opens the manila file in front of him. "Can I show you something?" he asks. He passes some printouts across the table. She understands what he is doing: he is fully invested in humanizing himself. What else did she expect? Even the worst of humans demand a portion of love.

She fingers through the photos. Her heart vaults. His three young daughters. They are extraordinarily beautiful. They wear bright dresses: baby blue and pink. Their hair is neatly combed and braided. The photo is a close-up, and she wonders aloud where it might have been taken. "In the camp," he says, almost impatiently: meaning the refugee camp, meaning Syria, meaning barbed wire, meaning armed guards.

He tells her that he has never seen his three-year-old in real life. He was captured before she was born. He does not show the face of his wife: it goes against his religion, he says.

"They're beautiful," says Diane. She cannot help herself. She does not want to appear soft or open to easy manipulation, but it is true: the sight of them stalls her breath. And yet what sort of childhood might that be, amid the tents, the hanging clotheslines, the hunger, the whip of wind?

Another photo is slid across the table. His 18-year-old daughter from England, a child he left behind years ago. She is aware of the pulsing strangeness of the moment: the man accused of conspiring to kill her son is showing her pictures of his own living children, even the one he has abandoned.

He receives the copies back from across the table, holds

them a moment longer. "Thank you," he says.

He is, he says, interested in honesty, compassion, charity, patience, abstinence, mindful knowing. The list surprises her. *Mindful knowing.* It is not a language that seems to belong to him. But he has, she knows, had access to a counsellor in recent weeks and perhaps he is learning to echo what others might want to hear. He says he is not sure what he is going to do with all these things, but he will one day face his Lord.

Face his Lord. The thought of it brings a shiver along her forearms. She beseeches her own.

In the room, the clocks tick, unseen.

It has been a day of shadows and redirection, revelation and lies. She gets the vague sense that Kotey—with his confidence and his silence—might think himself to be the smartest person in the room. He is intelligent yes, but it's an intelligence that needs to wear a disguise. And besides, the smartest person in the room is the one who knows she, or he, is never the smartest at all: herein lies the contradiction. She wonders now if he has just said exactly the things she wanted to hear? She knows herself to be naïve at times: she admits this to herself. Yes, it is true, she has often been far too open to people in the past. She has been stung. Government officials who have deceived her. Pretenders from the FBI. Misdirection from the State Department and White House. Politicians. Negotiators. Informers. Conmen. And, perhaps now, Kotey. But she knows that naïveté is necessary to cultivate something deeper. She wants to remain open to the world. *Compassion, Lord. And mercy. And patience.*

There will be one more session tomorrow. Perhaps they will achieve something more than this intimate stand-off. But then again, perhaps nothing.

She pulls back her chair and thanks him. It is dangerous, she knows, to thank him. But she must do it anyway. Perhaps it's only politeness. Perhaps it's something more.

"In another life," she says, "you and Jim might have been friends."

She spends the evening with friends in D.C. Over a bouillabaisse stew and a single glass of white wine. It's a quiet night and there is much talk about: Jim's legacy foundation, its finances, the fundraisers, the hiring of a new director.

When the talk turns to Kotey, another shiver of cold goes along her spine. There is something undone about the day. She can't quite locate what it is, but she is glad that she will have another chance to talk with him. And there will be news, too, about Kotey's co-defendant, El Shafee Elsheikh—Jihadi Ringo, the media are calling him—who has not yet, in the parlance, copped a plea. The rumor is that he might go all the way to trial.

There is a bone-weariness in her. It was so exhausting to sit in front of Kotey for five hours. To know he was lying. To know he had not expressed any real, true remorse. To know that he had tried to minimize his part in it all. To know that he had distanced himself from the violence. To sense an edge of the psychotic to his denial. And yet for him to have opened up to her too, with the photographs, the smile, the open hands. It tore a rim at the edge of her heart. Was it all play-acting? Was it all just lies? There had been elements of charm about him, suggestions of honesty too. It had all whittled her down, confused her further. Yet she knew, when she had arranged to meet him, that she would be confused. To be confused was to be open to the possible. It was not hatred she harbored for him. Nothing at all like hatred. Nor anger. Nor mercy. She had not yet found a language for it.

Perhaps it is just time to go back to the real work—the administration of her foundation, the advocacy for other hostages, the caretaking of her elderly mother, the provision for grandchildren, an afternoon of quiet at home with John, an email exchange with philanthropists: the real work, on the ground, at eye level with a different reality.

Alexanda, Kotey, Mr. Kotey, Alexe, Alex, they are—all of him, every one of him—guilty. He has admitted it. He will spend his whole life behind bars. And so what is the point in reaching him now? All the fear, all the anger: seven long years. Sometimes she fears that hers is a naïve, simple-minded way of seeing. Perhaps she should put all this prison pageantry aside? She wonders if she has invested too much time in it all. Should she just have remained what she once was—a nurse, a mother, a housewife, a grandmother?

There were others out there who have called her a saint, of all things: *a saint*. She has heard it quite a few times, and it bothers her deeply, brings a flush of embarrassment to her cheeks. There is, for her, a sort of shame in that admiration. She is, she knows, anything but saintly. Her son had been murdered. She has called for justice. She began a foundation for the return of other hostages. It was the only thing that she could do. Nothing saintly about that at all. Far from it. It was just one of the things that keeps Jim in the front of her mind. Every minute of every day. She cannot close the curtains of his life. She is a mother. That is all, and that is more than enough.

A late-night taxi takes her home through D.C., past the White House, out towards the quiet streets of Alexandria, where Kotey sits in his jail cell.

In the hotel lobby she is acknowledged by the staff. Over the past two days, she has learned so many of their first names. Not only that, but she has remembered their names. They nod and smile at her as she passes through. There is something about this woman: she stands out and yet she also fits in, an everywoman, yet unique.

She adjusts her Covid mask, presses the elevator button.

In the room she slips wearily beneath the sheets. Her phone has rung several times over the course of the night. But she calls John before she falls asleep: he has been looking after two of their grandchildren.

"Hi, honey," she says. "How are the kids?"

It begins rainy and cold. A gray gauze hanging over the day. It is a short umbrella'd walk from the hotel to the Department of Justice. The prosecutors are waiting for her on the third floor. These people are, she feels, the best of American justice. The years after Jim was captured were pure debacle—the FBI with their hands tied, the stonewalling, the opportunities missed by the Obama administration—but, in this case, the Justice Department has guided her well. In particular, Dennis Fitzpatrick, the assistant U.S. attorney, her go-to contact, along with Jenn Donnarumma, victim witness specialist, and Acting U.S. Attorney Raj Parekh. They have been careful. Kind. Meticulous. Beseeching. Compassionate. Mindful. They have not wanted to turn justice into revenge. They have protected the interests of the families. Understood their desires. Saw the larger landscape. And they have achieved—at least with Kotey—a life sentence.

They greet her with the news that Elsheikh, the other of the three Beatles, in jail just down the road, has refused a plea deal, meaning he will go to trial in a few months. It brings a sigh to her soul. Nothing ever ends really. But perhaps something good can come out of it.

Kotey is waiting in the same large windowless room. She pulls up the chair and leans in close to the table.

"Good morning, Alexanda, did you sleep well?"

He nods, cradles his hands around a paper coffee cup.

She feels a little more at ease today. She has slept a few hours. She needs answers to help her in the wider work against hostage-taking. She wants to talk to him, at first, about the definition of a combatant, the injustices against aid workers and journalists in the Islamic State, the targeting of innocents. "How does Allah feel," she asks, "about the killing of non-combatants?" "How does that square with Islamic philosophy?" "Why did you target journalists?" "What about aid workers?" After all, they carried no guns, she says. They meant no harm. They were only there to bear witness. Why were they so brutally pinpointed? Was bearing witness a threat to the Islamic State? What, she then asks, about people who were protected when they travelled with Muslims? Should they not have been protected? Why would anyone believe that you might act in good faith? Who, by definition, was protected? What—if like Jim himself—the hostages had embraced Islam during their captivity? Where did the covenants come in?

Kotey squares her in the eye. "Back then," he says, "I didn't question these things, I just went ahead and did them. Now, I question them so much more than I ever did before." In particular, under the laws of Islam and war, he says he has personally contested the morality of kidnapping aid workers and journalists, especially those who had converted to Islam. He admits to being ashamed and embarrassed by some of the things he has done. He can see himself, in another life, as a journalist.

"What type of journalist?"

"An impartial one."

"Like Jim."

Kotey simply nods.

There is something less imposing about him today, she thinks. He has dissolved a portion of that frozen wall.

"You said yesterday that Jim was an optimist. Are you an optimist, Alexanda?"

"I think I am a realist."

"What do you mean?"

"I want to be an agent for good. I will make my reparations. From Allah I will seek forgiveness for my wrongdoings, known and unknown."

"You believe in a merciful God," she says.

"I have confidence in my Creator," he says. "He will be there for my redemption. I understand His infinite mercy."

"God gives me solace too," she says.

He, she knows, has had time to study his Quran, the hadiths, the oral traditions, the laws. He has, like so many converts, the energy of the zealot, and he shuttles his truth into the territory of God, but he also says: "I don't sit before you now as a representative of the Islamic State." He talks of actions taken justly or unjustly. He has never supported the idea of suicide bombings. Of the beheadings he says: "I was against broadcasting them and making a media spectacle of them."

"Why was Jim singled out for the worst beatings?"

"I would dispute that," he says. "The worst was Daniel. Daniel was the fittest of the lot."

Daniel Rye Otteson. The Danish photojournalist who spent months in captivity with Jim and was later released. It was Emwazi, he suggests again, who took it out the most on James.

"I am sorry," he says, "for what you went through."

There is a silence in the room for a moment: it is heavy and held.

So, he is sorry. He is sorry. But only sorry for what she went through. Not sorry for what he has done. A slice of sorrow. A qualified sorrow. A sorrow verging on the cheap. But a sorrow all the same.

It strikes her that even if she hears nothing more from him, she will at least have heard that. An approach at admission. An approach at remorse. Even if was tamped down, mannered, qualified.

"You wrote Jim's last note. The 'Message to America' he had to read out before he was killed?"

"Yes. I was at home. On a computer. I wrote it a few nights before."

"Did it bother you?"

"It was what I had to do."

"And you said yesterday that you were not present at the execution?"

"I was at home with my family."

"And how did you feel?"

"At the time it was war."

In a bare apartment. On the outskirts of Raqqa. A sofa, say. A few chairs. A mobile phone buzzing on the table. The children and his wife in the next room. The sound of distant explosions. He rubs his fingers through his long beard and types: *I call on my friends, family and loved ones to rise up against my real killers—the U.S. government—for what will happen to me is only a result of their complacent criminality.* He finishes the message. He saves the file. He closes the computer. He again strokes his beard. Later that same day, a knock on the door. Emwazi enters. Kotey shares the file with him. It is, essentially, a death warrant, another edge of the blade.

It is odd to look at his hands, here, now, in this moment, many years later, this man who wrote her son's last words. Was he there in the desert for the execution? Was he not? What is the truth? But what is the point in knowing the truth at this point anyway? They can continue circling around a dozen different truths and each time it will emerge shaded differently. There are so many forms of the truth. The truth, she knows, is an ongoing enquiry into itself.

"You said yesterday that you watched the documentary?"

"Twice."

"And what did you think?"

"I had mixed feelings about it."

He continues kneading his hands.

"I didn't feel guilty," he says, "but I felt compassion."

"Why?"

Another silence, then in the room. *Jim: the James Foley Story* was directed by Jim's boyhood friend Brian Oakes. She was initially against the project, thinking it intrusive, but she came to admire the film, its bravery, its construction, its honesty: it captured her son perfectly, even discovered things about him she had not known. But she is curious as to how—and deeply why—Kotey might have watched the film a second time. What sort of instinct could have led him to watch it again? Was it perversity? Or simple curiosity? Or gloating? Or a way to know his enemy? A way to transcend perception? Why did it cut so sharply under his skin?

"It was emotional to see your family's emotion," he says. "Especially James's father and how it affected him. It got to me."

She recalls the scene: her husband John in the living room, heaving with tears.

Kotey pulls his feet in under the chair. He curls and makes himself smaller. A strange sound seems to come from a distance. Something guttural, something clamped. And she realizes then that it is coming from him, not from her memory.

She looks along the length of the table. There are seven other people present in the room. But there is only this one human sound. And then it happens again. She can see him fighting to hold it back. She is sure that it is not rehearsed. It happens again. His head so deeply bowed. The last thing she had expected from him.

Tissues have been placed on her side of the table for the

past two days. Her family friend leans across. So too does another observer. Kotey opens the package.

Another long silence. Then he catches himself, wipes his eyes. He shakes his head to snap himself out. Hauls in a net of breath.

"Because I also felt a resentment, you understand?"

"I think so," she says.

A resentment, she wonders. What resentment?

"Can I tell you a story?" says Kotey.

"Yes."

What he tells, then, is haphazard. It has no dates. No specific geography. It is related in a staccato manner. One detail to the next. Suggesting to her a truth. There is no rehearsal here. The story comes in fits and starts. He talks about a Canadian mother and her one-year-old child. He was out with a friend of his, he says. They were somewhere engaged in battle. A British fighter too. A friend of his from the U.K. This fighter, this friend, lived on the outskirts of the city. "We were coming back from battle. His wife and daughter, you see? What happened was a drone strike, you understand? An American drone strike. A specific attack. With no warning. They chose that building. Where they lived." His eyes are closed as he speaks. "And one half of the building was still standing, and the other half was just gone, just blown away, demolished. We ran to it. My friend and I. His family were there, see? And we started searching through the rubble, picking things up, things, bits and pieces. One woman was alive." A vacuum of silence in the room. "And then we found them. But they were dead, see? I pulled out his little baby from the rubble. She had nothing to do with it. A year old. One year old. You understand? They weren't at war. Collateral damage. That's what your government said. We carried them through the streets. To bury them. I was beyond emotion. You could have hit me with a million drone strikes, I would not have cared, you understand?"

She does not want to dismiss his story. It confuses her but pierces her too: "The people need to hear these things, Alexandra, yes."

"And I was resentful, see, when I saw the documentary. Because nobody got to tell her story. Also because I was affected by James's story too. And his father. I was ashamed. I should have reserved my grief, you understand? But James gets his story told on HBO. He's white and he's American. People listen to him. But nobody told her story, that child." He breathes in another net of air. "Because she's not white and she's not American."

His, briefly, is a one-hundred-yard stare.

"But you could have told her story, Alexandra."

He gathers himself. Puts his clasped hands to his forehead, dries his eyes with his fist: *that fist*. She knows, too, what he must be thinking: How could he have told that story? Who would have listened? By what means could he have told it?

It will, she knows, be almost impossible to tell others— her family, her friends—about this moment. Hard to believe that the man who tortured her son is sobbing no more than four feet in front of her. Hard to explain that it is, most likely, not an act. Hard to illustrate how she has contained her emotions. Hard to judge if he is exploiting the moment. Even harder to explain that it is not just the story of a one-year-old child taken from the rubble, or a father crying in a documentary, or an anonymous drone strike, or a tortured son, or a journey across mountains, or a screed of hatred, or a tower coming down, or a city filled suddenly with poison gas, or a scorched earth, or a peddling of fear, or three young children in front a camera in a refugee camp, or a man who ventured out from New Hampshire, or a soldier who guided a remote drone, or a politician sitting in a suddenly small office, or a woman in East London edging her fingers along a photograph, or a six-year-old wondering about his uncle, or a chain hanging in the air of a basement in Abu Ghraib, or a blow of a steel pipe against the bottom of a pair of feet in Raffa, or the thud of a fist in the kidneys, or a murdered messenger, or the incanted prayers, or the way it is all knitted together, from Wisconsin to London to Damascus to New Hampshire to Tripoli to Virginia, all these wild and braided things, somehow held together and not by language: there is no word for it that she knows of. She beseeches the Holy Spirit to come down and help her find one. *Give me mercy. Give me strength.* Maybe it is not enough to say that it's just sad, it's all just sad, it's terribly sad, but perhaps there is no other word, just simple sadness that Jim is dead, and sadness that Alexanda will spend the rest of his life in prison, and sadness that his daughter in England will never know him, and sadness that Jim's nephews will not see him at Christmas, and sadness that so many people want to poison it with narrowness, and sadness that others want to turn away and forget it all, and sadness that nobody wants to know about the hostages, and sadness that the newspapers and television stations and websites are struck dumb by indifference, and sadness that nobody knows what innocence means anymore, and sadness that we still go about taking the lives from one another, and sadness that it comes down to either justice or revenge—as if that is the only choice—and sadness, too, that the very sadness itself is not an answer.

She knows that she will be called naïve if she tells the story, somehow, someday, on television somewhere, or in print, or on the internet—they will say that she was duped by him, that she fell for his act, that she allowed herself to open up to his deception, but it doesn't matter, not a bit, not in this moment, no.

Diane Foley allows herself for the first time, the very first time, the only time—since August 19th, 2014, the day her son's death was announced—to cry in public.

She does not make a spectacle of it. She does it quietly. Hardly anyone in the room knows. She is not even sure that Alexanda, four feet across the table, knows. She brings a knuckle to her cheek.

Seven years. No distance between then and now.

"I hope one day we can forgive one another," she says to Kotey.

He is taken aback: "There is no reason for you to offer forgiveness."

───────────────

She spends the rest of the day travelling. An Uber to Reagan Airport. A flight to Boston. A car trip to her daughter's home to help with Colin, the newborn. She arrives late at night. It is almost Halloween. The car brims with cornstalks and pumpkins and flyers left over from the recent Foley Freedom Run. She holds the swaddled child. This, then, is what matters. A warm new life in her arms.

Two days later she is at her mother's apartment in New Hampshire to cook and clean, dose her medications, and bring her to Sunday Mass. And then it is time to join with John and five of their grandchildren to go trick or treating. The streets full of ghosts.

It has taken her a while to consider what has happened in Virginia. She had doubted Kotey, yes. She didn't believe all his answers. She was quite sure that he had done terrible things. He had beaten Jim far more than he admitted. And he had beaten others—savagely, she was sure of it. He had deceived himself into believing that he was not fully culpable. He had probably lied to her: he was possibly present for the day of execution. But the truth was that anyone in his situation would have lied, or at the very least tried to shape the truth. And every truth is eventually shaped. He was looking down the barrel of time. Facing the rest of his life in prison. He had to carve a narrative for himself. He would have to be able to live inside his body and his memory too. He had said at one stage that he had stopped living for himself when he had children. He wanted them to grow up, marry, have families of their own. A simple wish, but one that he would never experience. He had called on her to understand that one moment. The child. The rubble. There was no such thing as collateral damage. He had done what he had done for the reasons he had enumerated. It was this that had that sent that familiar rush of cold along her spine. People needed to know. And there was still the only word she could return to: sadness.

He had not apologized to her, no, but she saw in him she wasn't yet sure what. His accountability perhaps? That, she could admire. Yes, he had been accountable for what he had done, or at least what he admitted to doing. She found compassion for him too. A sort of understanding. He aspired, he said, to be an agent for good. That was simplistic, of course, but even the simple, or maybe especially the simple, can sometimes run the course of truth. He had pointed out the cycle of violence. Who could understand the tangle of history? Who was to say where humility begins and hatred ends? Kotey would die in jail. In shackles. In a small room. He would probably not ever see his daughters. He would hold the photos and he would sharpen the memory, but that was all. That, too, was tragic.

In the end, her own tears had been more surprising—even to her—than his.

It was the Holy Spirit that was present for those awkward hours of conversation, she was sure of it. The tears had been a gift. She had been released. She was quite sure Jim had been sitting alongside her. He sat his long, lanky frame beside her and looked Kotey straight in the eye.

She had told Kotey, just before she left, that she would keep him in her prayers and that maybe he too could keep Jim in his own prayers. Then she rose and bid him goodbye.

Seven years. It was time to heal.

Time to tell her story.

BOOK TWO

1

If I Should Close My Eyes

August 2014

It was a Tuesday afternoon in the middle of August in our home in Rochester, New Hampshire. Three of us were sitting at the round white kitchen table, drinking coffee, keeping up on the news, chatting—my sister Rita was visiting from Texas, and my husband, John, had stayed home from work.

It had been one of those lazy summer mornings under a blue sky, birds chirping, a nice breeze coming in through the open window. Our old cat Missy was curled up in the corner of the kitchen waiting for nothing to happen.

My cell phone rang. It wasn't a number I recognized, but it wasn't unusual to get a random call. Jim had already been held hostage for almost two years. It could be a journalist looking for a quote, or a federal official with an update, or a friend calling from a number that wasn't in my contacts. Of course, every phone call also came with a thump of the heart. It might be THE call with news that Jim had escaped and broken free. Or maybe someone had managed to contact the hostage-takers and there was a breakthrough, or their demands had changed. Or there was a development, maybe even a peace agreement, a step on the road to reconciliation, some peaceful end to this madness.

We had remained hopeful all those long months, living with the prospect of darkness but positioning ourselves in whatever light we could find. We awaited an email. A phone call. A flight to be arranged for him and his fellow hostages to come home. A welcoming committee at the airport. A scrum of journalists and family and friends. Someone to untie the yellow ribbons from the trees on our street. We would watch Jim walk into the house, his broad grin leading the way, and we would embrace the reality of the possible hidden within the impossible.

"Hello."

There was a brief silence on the other end, and then what sounded like sobbing. I must have thought that it was a prank or a robocall, but then the intake of breath on the other end made itself apparent, and the voice announced herself as "Lara Jakes" from the Associated Press. I could not make out exactly what she was trying to say—it had something to do with Twitter. Had I had seen a tweet? I have no recollection of what I said to her as she sobbed, but she caught herself and said that she was sorry, but please look at Twitter, she would call back in a few moments.

And then she hung up. I looked at the phone. I looked at the sink. A drip came from the kitchen faucet. I saw it clear as light. It hovered a moment and then fell.

At 3:45 Rita's phone rang. It was her husband, Fernando. He was one of the administrators of the "Find Jim Foley" Facebook page. My sister handed me her phone. Someone had posted an image of our Jim on the page, he said. He wasn't sure if it was real or not. I asked Fernando to send me the link. An ache of time went by, possibly only seconds long. The link arrived. I clicked through on my laptop. It led to another link. I clicked again. Then again. It didn't seem possible. A desert landscape. An orange jumpsuit. A man in black, only his eyes apparent. "A Message to America."

Time didn't just freeze: time disappeared entirely from time.

There was my son—or someone who looked like my son— with his bloodied head upon his back.

I didn't cry, didn't even turn my head away from the horror. This had to be photoshopped. A cruel prank. It couldn't be real. The impossible could not have actually occurred. Not now. Not this way. It was still just an ordinary Tuesday. The sky was blue. There were birds in the air. There was lunch to prepare. My granddaughter's birthday to celebrate. News like this could not arrive on a day like this.

Two weeks previously, ISIS had sent an ominous email threatening to kill Jim if the bombing in response to the massacre of the Yazidis in northern Syria did not stop. But they had threatened this same thing many times before, and the FBI assured us it was just another idle threat. It was part of their *modus operandi*. They were masters of deceit. They had performed multiple mock executions. Surely this was just another ploy. Jim had likely been taken out into the desert and made to kneel and they had pretended to slice a knife across his throat and then they had manipulated the image, photoshopped it, and here it was now, in front of our eyes, in front of the world, a gratuitous lie, incredible in every degree.

I frantically started emailing and phoning any and every government official I knew. Nobody replied. Surely some agents would come knocking at the door at any moment? Surely, if it was true, we would have had some sort of official communication? I was in a daze. This could not be happening. We had prayed so hard for Jim's safe return. It couldn't be turning out this way.

Not our Jim. Not now. Not ever.

A pair of Boston-based FBI agents had appeared at our house earlier that morning. Two smartly dressed women had pulled up in a car outside. We were sitting on our back porch enjoying the incredible sunlight as it poured down. Unexpected, unannounced, they had walked up the driveway. The clothes they wore disguised the guns they carried. They were not aloof, but clearly they were not interested in conversation. They wanted Jim's DNA, they said. We wanted to know why. They were kind but insistent. "We just need it for records," they said.

John and I looked at each other: why after two years did the FBI suddenly need our son's DNA?

We sat on our screened back porch while they swabbed the inside of our mouths. They took the cotton swabs and sealed them in bags with surgical care.

I offered them tea or coffee. They didn't want any. Instead, they wanted to know if there was anything of Jim's DNA left in the house. His DNA was in the very air of everything, I wanted to say. They would find snippets of James Wright Foley throughout the house, asking questions, making us laugh, telling us stories. I stood up from the porch, went inside and down the steep steps to the dark basement where Jim had stored his belongings the last time he was home.

Four trunks. One old cedar trunk and three big black plastic bins. I opened them up, rifled through them. Jim had never owned a lot of things. He wasn't really interested in belongings. There were his plaid shirts, his flannels, his rugby shirt from Marquette University. Some camera equipment. His cherished books. Some of his papers. An old woolen knit hat in the shape of a football helmet.

In a dopp kit I found a toothbrush and toothpaste neatly wrapped in a plastic bag. It hadn't been used in years, but it would still harbor his DNA.

The alarm bells weren't ringing, or at least they weren't making a racket in my head. It was an unusual request, yes, but I had come to consider the unusual as a regular guest in our lives. Jim would be coming back to fill these shirts and read these books and wear this silly yellow hat again. Before going upstairs again, I replaced the hat on top of the pile. Even in his absence Jim could make you smile.

The FBI agents took the toothbrush and left us sitting there wondering what had just happened. Maybe they knew something and were operating in advance. Or maybe they were just a couple of years too late.

After the image was posted on Twitter, the day passed in a blur of phone calls and messages. Phil Balboni, co-owner of *GlobalPost* in Boston, the online international news agency which had employed Jim on a freelance basis, was one of the first. Phil had engaged a security team to help bring Jim home and he had been calling us on a weekly basis with updates. The news seemed to have hit him with the force of an axe. He sounded like he was speaking from underwater when he said to John: "Jim has been murdered."

I still didn't want to believe it. Once again, I emailed everyone I knew in the U.S. government from the FBI agents to Susan Rice, the National Security advisor, but nobody got back to me. No messages were relayed through the local police. There was no announcement on the radio. And nothing official on the TV. Maybe the silence had a code inside it.

My mind was a riot of questions and doubts. Why had the two FBI agents come to the house earlier? Had they known something? Had they found out in advance of the actual act? Had the posting of the video been delayed?

Our son Michael arrived home late that afternoon. I hugged him at the door. He said that he'd had a candid conversation with Bill Heaney, an FBI agent we trusted, but nothing definitive had come out of that either. The family gathered around the table, still living in the realm of the possible. Surely all this would turn out to be a cruel hoax. It had to be. But when might the possible become impossible?

The phone buzzed incessantly, hour after hour. Our daughter Katie, a Navy nurse stationed in Norfolk, Virginia, would get home to be with us as soon as she possibly could. Mark, stationed at Joint Base Lewis-McChord near Tacoma,

Washington, was on his way as well. The FBI had arranged his flight. John Elliot, our middle son, and his family had just moved to Belgium in his role in the U.S. Air Force: he would do everything in his power to get home as soon as he could.

There was no single piece of absolute truth coming our way, but the suggestions were kaleidoscopic and beginning to fill us with dread. The phones buzzed again. *The New York Times.* The Associated Press. Our local paper, *Foster's Daily Democrat.* A Fox News truck pulled up outside our house. Reporters came with their inquisitive heads bowed. One eye open, the other eye open too.

Time had stopped. The clock hand moved, but time itself wouldn't move with it.

Questions came in swarms. If it were true, if Jim were dead, gone from us forever, how would I tell my mother? My grandchildren? *If* it were true. And if it was, to what degree had Jim suffered? What were his last words beyond those that he had been forced to recite to the camera? What had he gone through? Had he whispered a word to God? A plea? A supplication? His gratitude for what he'd been given? What were the final thoughts that went across his mind? How would we ever fill the void?

The kitchen began to fill. The house. The back porch. Shadows and shapes flittered on the front lawn. The world hummed. Murmurs and whispers closed in.

Then, late in the evening, suddenly, and not suddenly, it became horribly true. President Barack Obama announced on the news that Jim had been beheaded by ISIS in Syria, and nothing—not the birds outside, not the sunlight, not the dripping faucet, not the dark—none of it could rescue us from the flood of grief. The ache inside cannot be described except by its own pain. I was sundered, torn apart. Nothing had ever felt even remotely like this. Nothing. The pulverizing shock of hatred's power.

To lose a child is among the worst things that can happen to a parent. There's no specific word for it in the English language, nor in Spanish or in French or any other language for all I know. What word could capture and convey such loss? We have *orphans* and we have *widows* and we have *widowers*, but we have no language for a parent who loses their own child, maybe because it seems almost impossible to imagine. It goes against the grain of life. We are all supposed to pass along before our children even begin to flourish. Otherwise, we have to go on living knowing that a part of us has disappeared, unwillingly, unwittingly from the world.

I'd always considered myself a person who tries to find goodness in the darker places, an optimist, a woman of faith. I did not want to give up my fervent hope for Jim to come home. But now President Obama had confirmed my son's death on television. I sat in silence with a current of anger surging through me. It was anger directed against the deranged ISIS fighters who had done this, of course, but also an anger towards our own U.S. government, whom I'd felt had patronized and deceived us all by abandoning our citizens when they claimed to have not. We had still not received a phone call from any government official, and yet here was our president on the television announcing it to the world.

When I parted the curtains early the next morning, I

could see all the news trucks and police cars jammed along our street. The news trucks had giant satellite dishes on their roofs, beaming out to the entire world. The siren lights on the police cars twirled. An ambulance idled further down the street: why in the world would an ambulance be there except to tend to a house full of broken hearts?

A couple of very young boys in shorts and T-shirts rode in circles at the end of the block, like every kid of every generation, going all the way back to when Jim did the very same thing. Yes, that could have been Jim down there, circling with no hands on the bars, his knees and elbows skinned from elaborate falls. There he was, looking up at us, looking down on him. But Jim didn't wave. Not today.

The news people were gathered in tight groups, clutching coffee cups, chatting. Reporters with notebooks. Some of them held microphones: WMUR, PBS, CNN, NBC, ABC, BBC, Univision, Telemundo. I closed the curtains. I didn't want the cameras swinging my way. We knew we would have to make a statement at some stage, but what could we say? Nothing prepares you for properly responding to the unthinkable. We hadn't planned for any of this. Why couldn't they leave us in peace? Why did we have to endure a full court press hemming us in? And yet I knew how important it was for the media to be there. The story had to exist in the world. They were colleagues of Jim's, after all. It struck me then that he was among them. Here. This day, at this hour. In the vans, chatting with the technicians and the cameramen, sharing cigarettes and mulling rumors, trying to make sense of the catastrophe. He was in the police cars as well, drilling down gently for information, nodding as the air conditioner hummed. Jim was a journalist, after all. He believed in truth telling. He would have been out there on the street, looking in. Or, even more likely for Jim, he would have been across town, as a reporter, in downtown Rochester at a diner with the ordinary people of the day, the truck drivers, the construction workers, the factory workers, the store clerks, talking with them over eggs and strong coffee, gauging how they felt about what was going on in the world: ISIS this, and ISIL that, and Daesh here, the Whatdyamacallits there, these savages, these terrorists, those—godforbid—*ragheads*. Jim wouldn't flinch. He wouldn't like that language, not at all, but he wouldn't turn away from it. Jim knew that in order to know, we have to listen. Listening is the quiet soul of storytelling. And sometimes what we listen to is what we do not necessarily want to hear. But we have to hear it anyway. In order to confront it, it has to be heard. And Jim was a great listener. If anyone would have liked to be present to report on his own death it would have been Jim. Not to celebrate himself, or to mourn, but to get underneath the actual skin of it, the deep-down dark reality of what the world was becoming, and why.

Jim knew that so much of knowing who we are becoming is the ability to understand where we have been.

Downstairs, most of our family was already awake and in the kitchen. Our middle son John Elliot had arrived from Germany accompanied by two FBI victim assistants. Katie had driven all night in her old Honda all the way from Virginia. The smell of coffee drifted up the stairs. Toast, eggs, bacon. But who could eat now? How could anybody taste anything? There was also the faint crackle of a police radio from outside. I turned again towards the bed. John was gone, already downstairs, preparing things for people. That's what John was so good at: he liked to prepare the world for everyone else. I could tell already that was how he would be able to get through this. He would shoulder things for people. He would keep himself busy. He knew how to treat people with generosity. He was a doctor, after all, even if he wasn't always very good at treating himself. He drank too much, smoked too much, ate too much, and, at the same time, cared too much, embraced too much, wanted too much for the world. He was a brilliant doctor to everybody but himself. First at the coffee pot, first at the spatula, first to fill up the milk jug, first to ask if you needed anything else, first to lift your plate, first to refill the mug. But also first outside to find a corner of the porch and stare into the distance where he would, undoubtedly, still find Jim and that portion of despair that he, John, was harboring. But John would get through this. He had started out as an emergency room man. Now he was the sort of doctor who could guide a tense room full of people through their illnesses. At the end of the day, he might stand back, aloof, but everybody else would be saved. He would leave his own treatment until last. And I knew, too, that he would be beating himself up about one thing in particular: he had not saved Jim. He was a father through and through. *I should have said this, I should have done that, I shouldn't have taught him this, I should have foreseen that.*

But Jim was gone. That was the reality of the morning. That was the evidence that I would find when I parted the curtains again.

Out there, the cameras and the circling bikes and the idling ambulance and all the waiting questions.

At that moment, I did not see a way through. But I had done enough crying during the night for a lifetime. I had stood long enough at the window. It was time to go downstairs. I braced myself, asked God to come with me.

In the kitchen, the air itself was upset. I felt like I was moving through water. People were hugging, whispering, consoling one another. My elderly mother, at the counter, couldn't stop crying. There was no way through but to embrace ordinary tasks. Make more coffee. Pick up the dishes.

John touched my elbow, but I didn't want to be touched. I didn't want to know that I was real. The complications of the world were overwhelming. All emotions were in play. *Jim, James, Jimmy*: I heard his name everywhere.

We knew we had to leave the house and make a statement to the media at some point during the day. There was no way to avoid the truth. And yet we had to make something out of it. John and I were not interested in peddling sorrow. We had to carve something good out of this. It's what Jim would have wanted: but it was also what we knew we had to do. We had already spent a good deal of time with journalists while Jim had been in captivity, and they had interviewed us in several different situations. We had held a press conference in January of 2013 asking the world for help in bringing Jim home, but we found it hard to sustain the interest of the press during those endless months when there was simply no word of him.

We huddled in our small den discussing what—and what not—to say. Foremost, we needed to protect Steven Sotloff and the other remaining hostages in whatever way we could. Those who were living were the ones who mattered now. ISIS had threatened Steven and had shown his picture at the end of the video. They had said, in chilling terms, that he would be next, and that the blood would be on American hands, make no doubt about it. There was no need for us to inflame the situation with high-blown rhetoric or torrents of blame. If we could do anything at all, we might be able to take the temperature down. The country was at a boil already. We knew that. The internet was already howling out for revenge. There were calls for drone strikes. Pleas for special assassination squads. Some awful things were being said in the easy anonymity of Twitter. But even at that early moment I knew it wasn't revenge we desired.

I had cried when I heard the news but, now that it was real, we had to make something of our son's life. I resolved not to shed a public tear. We sent a message to the waiting journalists telling them we would have an impromptu press conference: just us, no representatives, no lawyers, no officials. John took my elbow, and we walked out the front door, onto the lawn, into the blinding August sunlight.

The cameras crowded in, so many of them, their little red buttons flickering with insistence. My husband slipped his arm around my waist. I wore my sunglasses, perhaps more to hide my eyes than to block out the sun. John was in shirtsleeves. It all felt so surreal, standing there like that, on our lawn, in front of our house, framed by the high trees in the background. I thought I might faint. I said something absurd to the journalists like "Thank you for waiting." John's cell phone went off three times during the live interview. It was a strange, high-pitched chirpy tune as if everything was okay. He didn't know how to turn it off until our son Mark stepped between us, took the cell phone and silenced it. How we would have liked to silence all phones, everywhere, across the world, at that particular moment.

But soon the proper words began to arrive. Jim was a courageous, fearless journalist, we said, the best of America, a hero to us. We had never been prouder of him. He gave his life trying to show the world the suffering of the Syrian people, to rouse our sympathy to action. We spoke of the memorized letter that had come out with a released hostage, and how those words had sustained us. We were bolstered by the fact that so many people were praying for Jim. John's words caught in his throat when he said that the last thing that Jim had said was that he wished he had more time to see his family.

"We pray that Jim's death can bring our country together in a stronger way," I said. "Jim would never want us to hate or be bitter. We will not do that. We are praying for the strength to love and to stay courageous. We thank Jim for all the joy he gave us. He was an extraordinary son, brother, journalist, and person."

We ended with the most important message of all, imploring the kidnappers to spare the lives of Steven and the remaining hostages. "They have no control over American policy in Iraq, Syria or anywhere in the world."

What I recall the most is that the journalists we knew—and many of the journalists we didn't know—listened with their heads bowed. Some cried, others stifled tears. It struck me then that it wasn't just one reporter who had been beheaded. The knife had been unsheathed to threaten all journalists everywhere. A debate had already emerged online about the ethics of showing the footage of Jim's execution. Why should anyone, anywhere, ever have to see that sort of thing? Once a thing is seen, it is so difficult to unsee.

The sun was still blazing, beating down, a relentlessness to it, maintaining the day as it was. I wondered when it was going to get dark.

———————————————————

The photo of Jim kneeling in the desert became iconic in a way that would always make us shiver. The world stood back in either stunned disbelief, or in perverted celebration at the sight of an empire wounded. Our country was rocked to the core. The murder was later seen as a pivotal moment in the recognition of the dangers of ISIS and their propaganda stunts. In fact, it was said that the image of Jim being killed was the second most recognizable image of the times, after the fall of the World Trade Center towers. A new front in the war had opened up. It was a propaganda battle which delighted in its own shock value. It wanted to inhabit every phone on earth, worm its way into public consciousness.

In the short term it shocked so many of us out of our stasis. Ordinary people wanted to do something, if even just to send a sympathy card our way to say: *We too are at your table, we share your grief, we are sorry for your loss.*

I still have some of the abundant plastic dinnerware that flooded into our house in those days. The food accumulated in the kitchen, delivered from work colleagues, concerned neighbors, local restaurants and a whole host of good people who cared. Chicken marsala. Vegetable soup. Chicken salad. Veal parmigiana.

Grief and empathy are sometimes hard to express, but food gathers us around a table, rallies us to try to articulate our remorse, not just for loved ones we have lost, but for a world that often seems to have gone awry.

In the weeks to come, whole buckets of mail arrived. Letters from all over the world. Mass cards, rosary beads, flowers. *We are praying for you. We are sorry for your loss. We are here for you.* Children's drawings. An Irish crystal candle base. Multiple portraits of Jim in oils and pastels were delivered to our doorstep. A stranger planted flowers around our mailbox. One day we received a huge 15-pound wooden cross engraved with Jim's name from an anonymous wood carver in Texas. There was a clock, a birdhouse, prayer shawls, three beautiful quilts. We received cards addressed only to "The Foley Family, U.S.A." Many of the letters included checks and donations to keep Jim's legacy alive. Already ideas of how to use the money were bubbling up in my mind. The generosity reinforced the reality of what had happened, but at the same time it was uplifting and healing too. The world showed itself capable of speaking up.

Still, it was difficult to force myself to eat in those days after. I knew I needed energy and focus, and that I could not afford to burn out. I did not want to be consumed by the feelings that were brewing inside me. I took long walks, trying to breathe myself free of a persistent tightness in my chest.

One thing I tried to figure out was the situation with the Obama administration. Their lack of outreach bothered me deeply and I tried to restrain myself from expressing that. At the best of times, I am impulsive and headstrong. I was seething, I admit. The president did not call until the third day after Jim's murder and by then I had allowed a portion of bitterness to creep in. His administration had always said that Jim was their highest priority, but I felt that if that were true then his captivity wouldn't have lasted two months, let alone two years. All the European hostages, bar the British, had been released. There was Marc Marginedas, for example, who had been incarcerated alongside Jim, as well as two other Spaniards, all of whom were quietly allowed back to Madrid six months before Jim's death. There were four French journalists released in mid-March. The Danish photojournalist Daniel Rye Otteson was let free in June 2014. On the day of his release, he called us to recite a letter from Jim that he dared not try to sneak out but had memorized by heart so he could share it with us.

If Spain could get their people back safely, why couldn't the U.S.? If France could do it, surely we could too. If the Danes could allow the families to raise money for their loved one's ransom, what was blocking our way? My grief snagged on missed possibilities. The sad truth was that I don't think our government had the will, or the desire, and that truth blocked Jim's way home. I later learned that Jim was never the administration's highest priority. Nor was any American hostage anywhere in the world, at any time, in any condition.

The administration was lying and—if they weren't actually lying—they were, in the very least, deceiving themselves into believing that they had made Jim a priority. The only one who was ever fully transparent with us was Colonel Mark Mitchell from the National Security Council, but that was a double-edged sword—he spoke plainly and with an unabashed candor, only to tell us that there would be no rescue mission to save the hostages, no foreign country would be asked to intervene, and we might face federal prosecution if we tried to raise a ransom to bring Jim home.

It would have been so much clearer and so much more elegant if the other officials had admitted the truth too. The reality was that they were not in the business of negotiating for hostages. It wasn't that they didn't care. Of course, they cared. That much was clear, and it is so important to say so. This is the essence of contradiction: they wanted a good outcome, but they did not do what was needed to be done to get the American hostages home. There was no malevolence on their part. They were open, and they were patriotic too. But they were hamstrung by bureaucracy, unprepared to embrace the policies that other countries had used. Hamstrung, too, by U.S. fears that negotiating with terrorists incentivizes hostage-taking.

Some of it was bravado. Britain and America would adopt the stiff upper lip. They would not kowtow to terrorism. They would not risk besmirching the pride of the military with compromise. There would be no concessions. They would not be seen to back down, even though other countries were known to pay for their hostages. And some of it was short-sighted economics too: after all, a single drone costs so much more than the release of a hostage, but nobody weighed up that equation. We send drones out into the world. For this we pay many millions of dollars—in fact the common Predator drone that the military used in Afghanistan and Iraq came, at that time, to $40 million per system. That's a lot of money. Our policy is that we know they might not come back. We accept that loss. But we do not want to negotiate for our living souls.

The bully in the playground is never subtle. Brute force is the easy answer. A good deal of the administration's behavior was short-sighted, if not cowardly. They were—or should I say *we* were—afraid that the terrorists would claim it as a victory, and nothing stings more in the American psyche than a public loss.

Also, the plain fact of the matter is that we don't care as much for our aid workers or our volunteer ambulance drivers or our journalists as we do for our military. Don't get me wrong—two of my other boys were in the military at the time, and my daughter was in the Navy. I have enormous respect for anyone who gives their life over to protect others. The people in the U.S. forces—and, in fact, the people in the Obama administration—put their lives on the line. This is the truth. There is a great selflessness about so much that is done by our armed forces and our diplomatic representatives. But the other plain fact of the matter was that the hostages, including Jim, were civilians, and civilians—even civilians bringing news of the war that our children were fighting—were a lot more expendable than the soldiers themselves.

If there had been twenty American Marines captured in northern Syria, I suspect we would have mounted a serious rescue operation. As we should. It is our military. They are on the very front lines. I am a patriot. All the America I ever need is always with me. But another part of me—the part that had to deal with the empty chair at our table—will never understand the willful neglect of our hostages. Jim went on a mission as a journalist to bear witness to the ground truth in Syria. Sure, he went there voluntarily. But surely risking one's life to present important moral and factual truths is as important as a military maneuver? Is an aid worker any less American, less essential, than a desk sergeant? Is an ambulance driver any less important than a Marine? And what happens when an American citizen goes in search of truth for the greater good? Is that not as patriotic as the actions of a soldier in a firefight?

To be a journalist is to seek the truth and share it. To go to the edge of who we are as a nation, as a people. That's what Jim had undertaken. In many senses he was a soldier too. He was a pacifist, putting his life at risk to play a significant part in shaping a world that is more aware, more caring, more profoundly in tune with others.

Of course, the argument can be made that these civilians and journalists went—and Jim certainly went—voluntarily. They put themselves at risk. It was their choice, and they took it. Nobody else should bear the responsibility for their well-being. But the fact is that they put themselves at risk for the truth, and what is the truth other than that which can save lives? All we have to do is think of the lessons of Vietnam. It took many years for the truth to emerge, but so many lives— Vietnamese and American and Cambodian—could have been saved if the truth-tellers had been listened to early on.

There are arguments and counterarguments, and we can continue spinning downwards until we hit rock bottom, but there was one indisputable fact: Jim and the other hostages were not our government's priority.

When the phone finally rang on that third day and we were told it was the president, a shiver of cold sluiced along my spine. I had respected and voted for President Obama. I believed him to be the right leader for our nation at the right time. I saw what progress could be accomplished under his guidance. But his administration had actually told us, in the coldest and starkest of terms, that the U.S. would not do a rescue mission, would not pay any ransom, and, furthermore, would not ask any other government anywhere around the world to help get Americans out. The chilling warning was the administration's way to get John and me and several other parents to back off from any idea of negotiation. It was even insinuated that we could be prosecuted if we were to try to take things into our own hands.

Now the president was on the phone. John went into the living room and took the call. I stood nearby, listening, paralyzed by expectation, anger and dread.

The president wanted to say that he was sorry for what had happened. John replied that Jim had been counting on the Obama administration to bring our son home. The president again said that he was sorry, and that he had done all that he could do. John said that our son Jim had gone out campaigning for him in 2008. The president responded with what felt like a genuine and reverential silence before saying that he appreciated that, he really did, he understood it to the core, but his administration had done all that it could. John replied that there was so much more that could have been done, and then the president told him that he had, in fact, ordered a top secret and extremely risky rescue mission into Syrian territory in early July, with our very best forces, but the site that they raided had already been abandoned, and the prisoners had been moved. John and I were unsure how to take this information. Politics and war are the most intricate incubators of lies, but at that moment we believed him. There had been a mission with some of our most elite troops, but it had failed. Our soldiers had been dropped down into Syrian territory, but the administration had waited too long, and our forces had come up empty-handed.

The phone quaked in John's hand, but he pushed on at an even keel. The call lasted no more than two or three minutes.

"Thank you, Mr. President."

And that was it. There was a finality to it. It was here, now, and it was undeniable—the president had called to communicate his sorrow for the loss of our son.

I later found out, watching CNN, that the president had almost immediately gone to a golf course on Martha's Vineyard where he was photographed laughing with his golf partners. Perhaps he had called us from the course itself. It bothered me, and it knocked me off-kilter, but I suppose I understood it. I knew that Obama had a nation to lead, and that nothing about his duty was simple. One of his great assets was his ability to hold several contradictory ideas in the palms of his hands all at once. He had also taken time off from his vacation to give a press conference about Jim the day before. His words, even if carefully shaped, had held the ring of the authentic. And there was so much that he had to hold together. So much to keep in mind. But I wished he hadn't made an announcement at a golf club and allowed himself to be photographed shortly afterwards.

If there is one thing I have learned over the years—especially since Jim's death—it is that there is no such thing as a singular truth. The truth is kaleidoscopic, it has many mirrors, and it can be viewed from a variety of angles. The best truth, the truest truth, is a cumulative one, a textural one. It has an ineffable core that might be hard to reach at times, and just as hard to understand, but it still has a center around which it rotates. And the core of the truth here was that something vile had been unleashed in the world, an organized evil, and a young American had been murdered by it in cold blood. Others were at risk. Eventually, I knew, there would have to be some sort of reckoning, some form of repair. At the time I had no idea from where the repair might possibly come.

Over the next few days, others who visited the house brought relief and a sense of purpose with them. There was our family, of course—our children, who were shocked, bewildered, grieving; my cherished mother, who could not stop sobbing; my beloved niece Meghan, my dear friend Beth, all of whom came along and offered support. Our local priest, Paul Gousse, came over to pray with us and give us solace.

We didn't want to walk out into that world of microphones and satellite dishes and questions. Still, we invited some trusted reporters into our home. Anderson Cooper sat in our living room with his producer at CNN, Allie Brennan, who so kindly brought me flowers. She wanted the world to know the truth in all its complexity. She felt a moral imperative to tell the story as it was. Greta Van Susteren from Fox News was also very kind, and we granted her an interview. I began to see the power of knowing what it was that I had to say. So much of it had to do with the other hostages and our government's policy towards our citizens. I hadn't yet decided for certain, but the idea of forming an organization to help the families of hostages began to float through my mind. If I was able to set my eyes on this, I might be able to live with the reality of this new life. Jim's sacrifice would mean something: he had always wanted to exist unselfishly, to make a difference for others.

On the fourth day a phone call came that left an indelible mark on me. I was in the kitchen with John and other family members. Our dear friend and priest, Marc Montminy, was alongside us. So too was my mother. The call—which had been scheduled through the Diocese of Manchester—came from

Pope Francis. It was all the more extraordinary since I had heard that the pope's beloved nephew, Emanuel Bergoglio, had been in a severe car accident, and that Emanuel had lost his wife and children.

We offered our condolences to the pope for his loss. Even from a distance we could sense the deep empathy of His Holiness. He thanked us, but really he wanted to speak about what had happened to Jim. He said that Jim was a martyr and that he would be remembered forever for the depth of his courage and his unrelenting commitment to the truth as a journalist. The pope's English was halting, so my brother-in-law Fernando took the rest of the call in Spanish.

Even in another language the Holy Father's beneficent spirit came through. I didn't need an interpreter to know what his call meant. There was a holiness in the world that tied us all together. I have believed this since I was a child and felt it profoundly now. It was not a time to lose faith. If anything, it was a time for us to recognize the depth of our beliefs and to recognize what that belief can do to bring us together.

I was deeply moved by the call. It bolstered me. I felt consoled. It tied the ground and the sky together: hard, earthly realities alongside the solace of God. And Pope Francis valued not only our son's life but Jim's profession, his journalism, too.

I felt a strange sense of release. If we could take heart from our desperation and sadness, it was that Jim's spirit was beginning to appear everywhere. He was not done doing what he'd set out to do. ISIS may have beheaded him, but they had also given him voice.

Hope and History Rhyme

The muffler fell off the car on the way to the hospital. It was 1973, and just about everything was loud at that time. There was the Vietnam war, and there was Watergate, and the ribbon was cut on the World Trade Center, and there was the space race, and there was the oil crisis too.

Then, lo and behold, there was our battered old Pontiac dropping its muffler, making its own clatter as we made our way to the Evanston hospital from our Chicago apartment for the birth of our first child.

It was a dark October evening, and the cold was whipping along Lake Shore Drive. The muffler stayed behind, clanking to the side of the highway as we drove on, announcing ourselves a little too loudly at the front of the hospital. I waddled in, hand to my stomach, while John tried to find a parking spot.

When he was born, James Wright Foley, all six pounds

and seven ounces of him, decided to contribute to the world's noise with a piercing wail of his own.

Though a cheerful baby, he was a very light sleeper, so there were to be more than a few restless nights in our small apartment.

John was interning at Cook County Hospital at that time, working around the clock. I took time off from my nursing job to look after our little bundle of energy and volume. I tucked him into a baby backpack and walked along Lake Shore Drive for hours on end.

They were good days, shined to brilliance by the clean wind off Lake Michigan, filling our lungs.

Like a lot of young couples, John and I were trying to figure out a life together on the fly. Back in college I'd contemplated life in a religious order or maybe a career in the Peace Corps. Then, suddenly, there was John, a charmer from the get-go. He still likes to tell people that he fell "wicked, wicked, wicked" in love with me when we met in freshman camp at the University of New Hampshire. I had the biggest smile he'd ever seen in his life, he said, not to mention "every tooth still in her head."

One time I broke my ribs tobogganing at Dartmouth College, and he told me later that he was the one who could hardly hold his breath when he saw me.

His diagnosis was love. Mine was too.

We were married on campus by the college chaplain, Father Vincent Lawless, in August, 1971. It's strange how certain people become a fulcrum in your college years. No story of John and mine would ever be complete without mention of Father Lawless. The priest had a malformed hand and, in fact, had almost been denied ordination because of it, but he flourished in his calling. He represented so much to us, not least the possibility of what can be done in the face of adversity. His presence on campus was strong and consistent and comforting—whether it be in fraternity houses or sporting events or simply chance meetings on walkways between classes. We often attended his folk Masses in the evenings after studying. He died a little more than a year after our wedding—on the altar, shockingly, and appropriately, enough. A heart attack. While saying Mass. I knew I would never forget him, his quiet charisma, his authenticity, his piercing blue gaze.

There are people like him who are a force for good. They strike a tuning fork in your chest, one that keeps vibrating through the years.

John and I could not afford a honeymoon. Instead, we put our wedding gifts in a U-Haul attached to our secondhand jalopy, a red Mercury Comet, and headed west, the backseat piled high with boxes. The car broke down on our wedding night and we had to stay in a little hole of a motel in Troy, New York. We got the car fixed in a couple of days, and the U-Haul clattered along. We were youngsters motoring into a future where John was going to become a doctor and I was going to try to support us along the way with my nursing job.

In West Des Moines, Iowa, I worked as a community health nurse, counseling young parents about maternity and their newborn babies. At the time I knew little of motherhood, but I learned and shared whatever I could. Nutritional advice, vaccinations, sleep and safety measures. In particular I was drawn to the single young mothers who were starting out life on their own. They had so little, these women—or girls, rather—who had grown up in poverty, in urban and rural neighborhoods. They had lived in a world that expected little from them, sometimes didn't even want to recognize them. They were handcuffed by poverty and yet they still dared to raise their new babies in the world. They might not always have been ready for what reality would throw at them, but they would get through it one way or the other. Theirs was a resilience I admired.

For me, helping struggling mothers adjust to caregiving affirmed my desire to have my own child.

When I think back on it all, now, in the long corridors of memory, Jim had an old-fashioned childhood. It wasn't exactly out of a magazine—life never really is—but it came close enough. For the next six years, we moved around from town to town. We hunkered down for a while in Worcester, Massachusetts, a very livable American city with parks and colleges and hospitals. John joined the U.S. Army Medical Corps. We had a stint in West Point, New York, biking out to the scenic overlook of the Hudson Valley where life was green and vibrant. Our family grew. We watched the kids play in the backyard of our house in Fort Sam Houston, Texas. Jim and his brother Michael would put on their coonskin hats and prance around the perimeter fence on imaginary horses, playing Davy Crockett at the Alamo. It was called "Cowboys and Indians" in those days: little did any of us know how the world would change.

We were going with the flow. Our middle son, John Elliot, was born just before our move back east, to Fort Dix, New Jersey. Then, soon after moving back to New Hampshire, Mark and Katie came along. Five kids. A house in the country. An American life.

In the end we put our roots down in New England. It was familiar soil for us. We settled in Wolfeboro, New Hampshire, a picturesque town on Lake Winnipesaukee, two hours north of Boston. Here, a wind combed the water. The snow fell gently. We felt safe there. We could leave our doors unlocked and our keys in the car ignitions. It was a quiet, caring town, a throwback to a simpler time.

The years rolled on, hectic and joyful. I loved being a mother. We had our small financial struggles, but there was always enough to put bread on the table. I thought of us as the sort of family held together with a strong glue: faith and love. They were solid days, by a lake, in the shadow of the mountains. I was a mother first; my career as a nurse could wait. John established his practice. Sure, we had our rough moments. Everyone does. My mind doesn't dwell on them.

My memory is decorated with simple moments—watching Jim follow his finger along a page as he learned to devour books, listening to Michael bounce his basketball in the driveway, watching John run in a kids triathlon, seeing Mark learn how to ride a bike, and finally the birth of our daughter Katie.

The world we had was more than enough.

Jim was curious about the world and that curiosity ran itself wild in books. He used a flashlight under the covers to read. We rarely found him without an open book in his hands, even when he was sitting in a seat at Fenway Park during a Red Sox game. History, adventure stories, fantasy. Tin Tin, the wandering French cartoon character, was, unsurprisingly, among his favorites. He liked the clean drawings and the action-packed adventures of the young Belgian reporter. The plots often drew upon themes of politics, history and culture, braided together in an adventure story. In some ways I think Jim, at a young age, was already dipping a toe into the allure of the nomadic life, shaping discovery into a story. That was Jim's territory. He enjoyed whatever he was involved in, and if he could squeeze a laugh out of it, all the better.

At the age of fourteen, Jim got a job pumping gas for the boats on the lake. I can still see him there, one foot on the dock, one foot on the boat, holding the boat close to shore, chatting away and laughing with the boaters. Later he washed dishes at the Cider Press, sold shoes at Miltners, and waited on customers at Black's paper store. Sometimes he had to babysit his younger siblings. He was seventeen years old and Katie was only two, so it was more than a little embarrassing for him with his friends, but he did what was asked of him. Afterwards he went out, and I presume he did what teenagers do just about everywhere: he skateboarded, he drank beer, he drove through stop lights, and he had his crushes.

Throughout it all, Jim reveled in being slightly goofy. He showed up at his senior prom in a baby blue tuxedo *so* baby blue it was as if he'd just flown out of a bird nest. Imagine his poor date! He was the one to clown about in class, hitch up his trousers and launch into a Charlie Chaplin walk. He and his high school buddies enjoyed "skitching," a frowned-upon winter "sport" where a snowmobile towed someone on skates, sneakers, or boots across the frozen lake. It was New England, after all. The stars were out and blazing, and evenings stretched out beyond midnight into the small hours.

When I recall those days, I can almost hear the car radios playing as the kids pulled into the driveway. Bruce Springsteen. Journey. Huey Lewis and the News. Then the snap of the car door and the shuffle of feet up the stairs to the relief of a mother who has stayed awake to hear just that.

The greatest joys come in hindsight. Rearview mirrors tend to be uncluttered. I love looking at old photo albums. I am fond of opening up the past and dwelling there a moment. It is a form of nostalgia, of course, but there's something about nostalgia that also puts a fine point on the here-and-now. We are the accumulation of where we have been.

When I look back on those days with my kids, I am happy that we had the chance to experience what amounted to an idyll, and I am grateful for how uncluttered those days return, decades later, where even in the darkness I can hold the memory of that clear light.

Jim worked hard at school, overcoming a tendency towards attention deficit disorder. He was in many ways a late bloomer. He didn't quite know what he wanted to do, but there was his love of reading and literature that seemed to point him in the direction of a classical education. When it came time for Jim to apply to college, I encouraged him to apply to Jesuit schools so he could gain a foundation in his faith alongside a classical education. At first he thought he wanted to be either in New York or Washington, and was thrilled when he got into Fordham, American, and Holy Cross. But with East

Coast tuitions very steep, he was intrigued when a letter from Marquette University dropped on the welcome mat of our house one day. *Dear James, We are happy to inform you ...*

He pondered the acceptance. Marquette excelled in the arts. Its Jesuit background promoted a culture of engagement and caring. This mattered to him. We knew without him telling us that he wanted to actively engage with the world on its terms. He wanted to understand his own privilege, how to share it, how to pass it on, to be, as the Jesuits say, "a person for others," or, as one of Marquette's mottos had it, to "Be the Difference." There was also a generous four-year scholarship involved, not to mention the fact that Milwaukee was a long, long way from New Hampshire, and neither his father nor I were likely to land on his doorstep. So that was it: he was to become a Marquette boy, a Warrior, a thousand miles from home.

A quick glance around, and Jim wasn't there anymore. Marquette became his home. Because it was so far away, and money was tight, he would return home only for Christmas and summer break. His many friends became family. He studied history and minored in Spanish and continued his passion for learning about other people and places through many elective courses. He played rugby, and I suspect he contributed admirably to Milwaukee's reputation as the beer-imbibing capital of the Midwest.

I will be the first one to say that a mother never knows—let's be honest, she never really *wants* to know—what went on in college. *Hear nothing, see nothing, say nothing.*

But now, looking back, I realize that it was a crucial time in Jim's life. To be mentally navigating a host of ideas. To be pushing at the edge of thought and action. Even the fact that he was gone from our daily lives was important. He maintained a link with us, of course, with a weekly phone call, but he was already more about the world than he was about us.

It's incredible, though, what you don't know about your own child. Maybe it's the same for every parent, but it struck John and me years later that we didn't really know Jim all that well, not in his entirety, until after he was gone, after he was dead. Not that Jim was a secretive person, or even that he had specific secrets to hide, it was more that he wasn't so interested in talking about himself. He was not the spindle on which the world turned. When he did come home, he seldom revealed what was going on. He lived, I suppose, a bit like a river or a stream. He was interested in getting to the ocean of others. The river could be slow and steady, settling down opposite you to listen to what you had to say. Or it could take on a fast, tumbling energy. When he came home from college, or from his first jobs, Jim didn't really want to talk about himself. The world outside was far more interesting. He was the sort of person who, if he had a mirror, he wouldn't stare into it, but break it in two in order to hold the pieces up against one another and create an infinity. There was something Franciscan about it: the rest of the world mattered. And so, from an early age, he was always there to enable other people's stories. Other people interested him. He wanted their ground truth.

I like to think that some seeds of faith had been planted in his childhood, but there is no sliver of doubt in my mind that his sense of social justice was born at Marquette: his fascination with where others came from, what brought them there, where they were going, and how they might get to a better place. He was fond of a Seamus Heaney quote: *History says, Don't hope/ On this side of the grave./ But then, once in a lifetime/ The longed-for tidal wave/ Of justice can rise up,/ And hope and history rhyme.* Jim's true interests were situated at that intersection. He took philosophy classes, creative writing, ethics, Spanish. He stared deep into his own country's history and came to realize what a privileged middle-class upbringing he'd had in rural New Hampshire, how lucky he had been, the sort of comfort he had been born into: the clapboard house, the picket fence, the intact family. He didn't want to shy away from the awareness of his own privilege. Jim was exposed to poverty and inequity in the inner-city schools of Milwaukee, where he was encouraged to tutor as a freshman, as part of the Marquette program. I can imagine him tutoring in the classroom, tall, a little tentative, and incredibly passionate at the same time. He felt for those kids. He recognized something in their eyes. He could align himself with them. He spoke with them in fluent Spanish but also, I'm sure, in a manner of fluent humility. One summer he went to Appalachia to build houses with Habitat for Humanity, and during another he did service work on an Indian Reservation in the Dakotas.

I am well aware of a mother's tendency to over-saint her child, especially one who is taken early. But I also believe that it is not just parents who rear a child: it is the world around them too.

So, Marquette—the teachers and his pals, the ethics of the school—helped build so much of what Jim was eventually to become. But his question for himself was: *What do I really want to do? What am I actually becoming?* He wasn't entirely sure. He was still a touch on the young side, not so much immature as inexperienced. The idealist in him was strong. He was a dreamer. I think he was slightly afraid of what the practical world might want from him. The liberal education had laid a solid groundwork, that's for sure, but where was he going to use it? The corporate mentality did not appeal to him. The IBMs or the AT&Ts of the world with their CEOs and CFOs and endless acronyms were not for him. The idea of sitting in an office tethered to a desk most of the day would have sent shivers through him.

Nor was he cut out for legal work, even though he and his friend Tom Durkin had—on a whim—taken the LSATs on a hungover Saturday morning and surprised themselves by getting top scores. They blamed their temporary legal brilliance on the Guinness and used what was left of it to figure out other ways to break into the world.

After graduating from Marquette, Jim joined Teach for America where he taught in a tough, inner-city middle school in Phoenix, Arizona. Every Sunday when he called home he told us what a terrible teacher he was. Just wasn't cut out for it, he said. The middle schoolers in his charge had been more than a little skeptical of this tall white guy from some faraway place, a *gringo* who couldn't possibly understand them. He'd have been awkward standing at the front of that classroom, stumbling over the material, trying to get his bearings as they challenged him with the force of their insolence and disregard. In his weekly calls home, he told us how discouraged he was becoming at his inability to get through to these kids. He said the students had started a "Hate Mr. Foley Club." That hurt, but he didn't give up. One afternoon he wore his crisp teacher's clothes right into the middle of a muddy football game. Later he offered to coach the basketball team—and they began to win. Still, he kept most of his successes to himself.

After his three year stint in the Teach for America program in Phoenix and Milwaukee, he applied to and was accepted into the Master of Fine Arts program at the University of Massachusetts, where he tried his hand at writing fiction. He started with short stories and wrote a novel for his thesis.

He never quite accessed the voice that he wanted in his fiction. I saw some of his short stories years later. They were good, but you could sense he was straining. Looking and not quite finding. Increasingly, he suspected and then knew that his text, his best subject, would be the real world: he just wasn't sure which part, where in it to go, how to tell it when he got there.

While in Holyoke, Massachusetts, unbeknownst to us, he taught English and writing at a care center for young unwed mothers hoping to earn their GEDs. He inspired them to share their stories, to be resilient and hopeful. He purchased the group's first recording devices so the women could tell their stories, make a record of them that could be shared widely. His initiative has now grown into a public broadcasting radio program with the University of Massachusetts. Jim never told us any of this. He apparently did not think it was such a big deal.

And so it was that our son spent much of his younger years in a fog of good intent. He got a tattoo on his shoulder, a line from Oscar Wilde: "We are all in the gutter, but some of us are looking at the stars." But how to reach them?

Something nagged at the back of his brain. So much of his life was about stories and storytelling. He loved sitting around and listening for another's truth. That was what lit him up from the inside out.

After completing his MFA in 2003, Jim moved back to Phoenix. "It was the only time in his life that I can remember him moving backwards," his friend Tom Durkin told me. "He wanted to continue work on his MFA thesis, *The Cow Head Revelations*, a novel which was set in Phoenix. But his return to Phoenix was not what he expected, and he was pretty much rudderless." The pair went off on a trip together and Tom suggested that Jim should get a job at the Cook County Boot Camp for young felons, which was run by Tom's father. "He was perfect for the job—still young, bilingual, with teaching experience in a tough environment," says Tom. "He flew in for the interview wearing oversized hip hop jeans with painted symbols and then promptly fell asleep while waiting for his interview. My father joked that he had a million-dollar resume and a ten-cent interview."

During his two and a half years at the Boot Camp, Jim started to drift away from writing fiction. He wanted to get to know his students. They were all convicted felons in the age range of 18 to 34. But he saw the value in their lives. He encouraged them to tell their own stories. In fact, when he moved on to pursue an MA in journalism, he already knew the first story that he wanted to write. "At the Boot Camp he had been working closely with two inmates," says Tom. "Their names were Andre Odom and Maurice Jackson, both in their late teens, convicted felons and self-described 'gangbangers.' Jim followed them through even after they were released from the camp. He went to the housing projects with them, hung around, got to know them, followed their progress. Jim had found the type of stories that he wanted to tell."

I can picture that even now—Jim wandering through the projects, listening, quietly observing, trying to make sense of a world that was underexposed in the wider media. It was as if he was developing a photograph of sorts, spreading out his words in an acid tray, figuring out the light and the dark and the shade.

Years later—after Jim was killed—John and I would realize that we got to know him from the stories of others. Everyone seemed to have a Jim story and we became the repositories for those stories. I take a sort of solace in this: we got to know him afterwards, and so he lived on. In a way we are still getting to know him.

Scientists say that the world is held together with atoms and, of course, it is. But it is also held together with stories.

The News of the World

I lived through the era of broadcast news when the respect for the Ted Koppels and Walter Cronkites of the world was astounding. We were shaped by the fact that there were three or four respected television stations that would tell us our news, and the news itself didn't differ wildly from one channel to the next. Yes, there were different slants, and maybe even slightly different politics to each channel, but generally the message was one where we could grasp the main truth, or at least what we *thought* was the main truth.

And then there were the print journalists and photographers. They were the ones investigating the news in even greater depth. They unearthed Watergate and exposed the My Lai massacre. They wrote exhaustive articles and provided photographs of what it meant to be poor in America. They took the time to get in under the hood and check the engine for what was going on in the world. Dorothea Lange and Robert Capa. Joan Didion. Robert Fisk. Woodward and Bernstein. They were respected and liked as genuine truth-tellers. Outlets such as *Time* and *Newsweek* magazines and the *The New York Times, The Boston Globe, The Philadelphia Inquirer* and *The Washington Post* all seemed to have a pretty firm grip on what was happening around us. Of course, not everybody wanted to hear the stories that these journalists wanted to tell, but there was a respect for the craft and the craftsperson too. It said something about who we were as a nation.

Henry Grunwald, the managing editor and then the editor-in-chief of *Time* magazine in the 70s and 80s, once wrote, "Journalism can never be silent: that is its greatest virtue and its greatest fault. It must speak, and speak immediately, while the echoes of wonder, the claims of triumph and the signs of horror are still in the air." He went on, then, to add: "Home is one's birthplace, ratified by memory."

For me, there was always a spirit of necessity about journalism—a ratified home—offering people "all the news that's fit to print." It seemed that journalists were always going to be protected, like there was an unspoken alliance with the general public that the truth was essential, and that the good reporter was going to unearth that truth come what may. They might get criticized or pushed around or even kicked out of a country, but they were always going to come back intact to file their stories.

For a long time, I had no real idea what the life of a "conflict journalist" was all about. Like everyone else, I only had vague images printed on my mind from years of watching the news on TV or reading the newspapers. Mostly my idea was of these men and women—mostly men—on the balconies of hotels or in the rubble of bombed-out streets, trying to explain a war that seemed so alien and senseless. In the background there might be noise of distant explosions or some tracer fire arcing across the sky. Sometimes the reporters wore flak jackets and helmets, but most of the time it seemed like they stood at a safe remove from the war they were trying to explain. I thought how brave they were to be there, but I also believed they were safe, that no harm could come to them, like there was some sort of forcefield around them, created out of a natural respect for their craft. That somehow the ABC or the BBC logo gave them protection, and nobody would dare to try to silence them or do them harm.

We felt sure that Jim, too, was going to be protected by the aura of the calling and the essential spirit of journalism itself. He had written a couple of very good investigative reports in the local realm, for smaller newspapers, but he wanted his life and his work to be broader—and he was drawn to injustice and, therefore, conflict. So much of the American story was a global story. His first major job in journalism was when, at the age of 34, he embedded with the Indiana National Guard in 2008. He joined the 76th Brigade just before their deployment from Fort Stewart, Georgia. That meant he might have to go to some risky areas, but the truth was that we were much more worried about Jim's siblings, John and Mark, who were deployed to Afghanistan and Iraq.

Jim's role as a non-combatant seemed far less risky in comparison. He had found a career he was passionate about. It seemed to give him a sense of meaning. It expanded his sense of ambition. He could combine his natural listening skills and his writing talent with his sense of social justice.

Before he left, he spent a few days at home. He looked

great. He was happy and excited and a little nervous. He had packed a small bag. Some shirts, some notebooks, some novels that he liked. And off he went.

It is also sadly true that, at the same time that Jim was struggling to find his voice, a tiny bit of rot had begun to crawl into the perception of journalists in America. Journalism was grappling with the increase of "free" news on the internet. There was a decrease in the sales of print journalism. One by one, local newspapers were shutting down. Even the larger papers were taking a hit. Media companies could employ fewer full-time journalists. The wider world was changing.

When the towers came down in 2001 our country was concussed. I'm a nurse. I know what happens with a blunt force injury. The skull is stopped by an impact. But the brain, surrounded by cerebral-spinal fluid continues its original motion and—boom!—the brain strikes the hard inside surface of the skull leading to a bruising and swelling, a tearing of blood vessels, and a profound injury to the nerves. This results, then, in a loss of consciousness, dizziness, blurred vision, memory problems and fatigue. Kind of like flying a jetliner into a skyscraper.

America—and much of the world—was immediately concussed when the attacks occurred. We were sent reeling. It doesn't take too much hindsight to see that the punch-drunk boxer came out in a lot of us afterwards.

Among the many things that suffered was the way we, as Americans, dealt with the truth and the stories that we wanted to tell about one another.

Journalists were among those who had doubt cast around them. Some of the stories they wrote about what was going on in Iraq and Iran after 9/11 were controversial. We at home wanted to see ourselves playing out the great American hero epic, but often our journalists weren't giving us that comforting story. They were telling the truth, but, as we all know, the truth sometimes hurts. In many countries journalists have been targeted for their fealty to truth. The murder of the messenger is a huge issue of our times.

I'm not sure who came up with the concept of the "embedded journalist"—whether it was the journalists themselves, or the military. It was probably a bit of both. The military most likely felt that it could at least control the journalist, and maybe even the message, if she or he were embedded with them. And the journalists—certainly Jim was among them—thought they were getting to the very edge of the story. He didn't just want to be at the edge, he wanted to become the edge. He believed that by embedding with the very people who were fighting the war and protecting this country, he could find a deep-down truth about the lives of the young men and women, not only on our side, but perhaps on the other side, or sides, too.

Jim was wary of being embedded, of course. He didn't want to feel that he was co-opted by the system. He had to be sanguine about it all. It was a case of either going with the National Guard or staying home. He was interested in why men and women chose to become soldiers and, by extension, what effect a conflict might have on the places that these soldiers went. He wanted to get to the heart of the matter. That meant he was fascinated by soldiers on the other side too. And what interested him most were the people who were caught in between.

I felt—and by and large, I was correct—that by being with the Indiana National Guard he would be protected. Besides, Jim knew a thing or two about what it meant to be in the military. At that time John Elliot was in the U.S. Air Force in Germany, Mark was at Fort Campbell in Kentucky, and Katie was a Navy nurse in Virginia. Both the boys had experienced intermittent deployment to Iraq and Afghanistan.

Jim was a pacifist, but at his core he was also a pragmatist. He knew a thing or two about military manners and—although he was later to violate those manners on a marijuana charge—he was respectful of the core military tenets.

I haven't heard too many stories about his initial days in Fort Stewart, but I imagine he was able to get on very well with the soldiers. Apparently, he called just about everyone "brother" or "bro." *Hey, brother. Good morning, bro. What's going on, brother?* The thing was, according to the soldiers who hung around with him, he really meant it: they were his brothers. Essentially, he got an up-close view of the culture of the Guard, and he began work which would primarily appear in three papers in Indiana—the *Post-Tribune*, the *Pharos-Tribune*, and the *News-Sentinel*—and through his blog which he called, fittingly, "A World of Troubles."

For a tagline in his blog he used the famous statement made by Carl von Clausewitz, the Prussian general and military theorist: "War is fought by human beings." And, simple as it may sound, war *is* fought by human beings. Even contemporary warfare. That was essential to Jim's way of seeing: he was interested in uncovering the humanity in some of the most inhumane situations.

He was shipped out to Camp Buehring in Kuwait and one of his first articles from there was a dramatic recreation of soldiers rescuing a pinned truck driver in an overturned tanker. He was not yet a seasoned journalist, but his reports from the front were incisive and smart, and soon he was getting articles into the *GlobalPost*, an online news organization that would become pivotal to his life.

He also began to realize the power of the camera working alongside the word. He taught himself the ropes, and became a cameraman, a photographer and a writer all rolled into one. He was very much the modern journalist: a video camera in his hand, a stills camera around his neck, a reporter's notebook in his breast pocket.

He travelled alongside these men and women from the Indiana National Guard, through Iraq and through Afghanistan, and he tried to capture their day-to-day reality: the firefights, the internal and external politics, their dreams and their tragedies, and, of course, the day-to-day drudgery too.

His first tour in Iraq lasted ten months. The blog was popular with military families back home. He posted several interviews with the soldiers, reassuring those at home that their loved ones were getting through. The imagination can play wild tricks on people, but Jim's solid and even-keeled reporting kept the families level-headed and at ease. Words reduced the absence.

The other reality that interested him was the lives of those that don't always get talked about, the supposedly anonymous who, for the most part, don't get written about. Perhaps that's what made Jim different to a lot of people in the military bureaucracy: he wanted to see things from a kaleidoscopic angle. Among the articles he wrote was one titled "The Price of an Iraqi Life," which followed the trials and tribulations of an Iraqi mother, Sabah, whose son Mohammed had been a member of the Sons of Iraq, a group of local armed civilians who were paid by the U.S. military to guard checkpoints in problem areas mostly within the Sunni triangle near Baghdad. Mohammed was killed on a mission and his mother was tasked with trying to get compensation for his life. In the article Jim depicts a U.S. master sergeant counting the money onto the desk in increments of $50 bills until there was $1,000 laid out on the table.

That, then, was the price of a life. Twenty bills.

I still find it shocking to think about, and I imagine that mother, in a trailer office, watching the bills being laid down on the table and the horrible sound of the final bill hitting the wood.

All mothers know that life cannot be bought. Nor can it ever be compensated. Sometimes I think Jim was telling his own story in advance.

Kunar Province. Afghanistan. 2011. We are inside a turret-mounted grenade launcher with the soldiers of Alpha Company, 2-327th Infantry. They are under attack. Inside the tank is claustrophobic. There's an impending sense that anything can happen. The camera swings. The infantryman is 19-years-old. In the frame, it's him and the washed-out sky. The thrap-thrap-thrap of bullets. The gunner shouts for ammo. A few moments later he is shot in the head—"ahhh, shit"—but he is saved by his helmet. It's all daze and confusion. "Stay low, man." "Is he all right?" "Give me that fucking gun!" His fellow soldiers help the 19 year old down from the turret. They bandage him then leap into position. The 19 year old stares at the patch of blood in his helmet. "Holy shit," he says. The camera swings again. The footage is raw and sharp. The soldiers go to help the driver of the convoy in front who got hit earlier. A bloody arm. A tire on fire. The soldiers shout into the radio. A body is rolled onto a stretcher. They scramble to carry the wounded back to safety. The sky is gray and ominous. In the evacuation vehicle the soldiers reel physically and mentally from the attack. "Goddamn." "Oh, brother." "I hope I got that tourniquet on tight enough." The camera turns towards the barred window of the vehicle. The road is lined with Afghan citizens, standing along a river in their long tunic shirts and head coverings. One of the soldiers says: "What are you smiling at, motherfucker?" Back at base the soldiers smoke cigarettes and contemplate the terror of their afternoon. "My hands were all numb and shit," says one of the soldiers, half-haunted, half-relieved. In the final shot, the driver who lost his arm is medevacked out to safety—the helicopter rises up from the ground and the dust stings the eyes of the remaining soldiers.

The story, "On Location: A firefight in Kunar Province," became a 2011 Webby Award honoree.

It was—and it is—a profound piece of journalism. No editorializing. No commentary. Just the facts. It was the hard truth, the ground truth, the misery of war. As the helicopter lifts off in the air, the final line is: "This is James Foley, for *GlobalPost*."

The bylines continued. Jim was exhilarated by the work. The folks back home needed to be told what was going on. In January 2011 he joined *Stars and Stripes*, a multi-media military news organization providing news to soldiers all around the world. *Stars and Stripes* had been operating since the First World War. He took a job as a reporter on a 13-month contract which would give him largely unfettered access to stories around the world. This was a good position since it meant he was a staff reporter at last.

But the good times wouldn't last for long.

In March 2011—just six months after he filmed the fighting in the Kunar Province, and three months after he joined his new employers—I was in Germany where our son John was headquartered for the Army. I had gone across to help look after John's children while his wife recovered from shoulder surgery. Looking after the grandchildren was the sort of thing I really enjoyed: it gave me a true purpose and quite frankly just made me happy.

Out of the blue, Jim showed up. Totally unexpected. He looked completely miserable and downtrodden.

"I have something I have to tell you," he said, his eyes downcast. Every mother knows the dread that comes along with that sentence, no matter how old your child happens to be. "I'm in trouble." He had been detained at Kandahar Airfield by U.S. military police who found marijuana in his backpack. He wasn't charged with any crime, but he had been immediately banned from visiting any U.S. military base in Afghanistan and shipped back to Germany where he was unceremoniously asked to resign.

Thirty-seven years old...and busted for weed.

My heart went out to Jim. He was deeply embarrassed and unabashedly apologetic. He was worried that the news might hurt the military career ambitions of his brother John. And not only that, but his great new journalistic break had just vanished in a puff of proverbial smoke.

I am convinced that is why Jim left so abruptly for Libya again in March 2011. He didn't tell us he was going. He didn't have a defined job or a visa. He just upped and left. Tied his boots and slung on his backpack. Maybe he was carrying some of his fresh wounds with him too. He wanted to show the world that he wasn't some sort of vagabond pothead—he was a serious journalist, and he was intent on telling the stories that mattered. The Arab Spring excited him. He wanted to witness the struggle for freedom up close. To drill down into the civilian side. It was the stories of ordinary people that he wanted to capture. But his decision to keep going into the heart of these war-torn areas made us very nervous. John Jr. told him: "If you go over there, you know, nobody is coming for you." The U.S. was bombing Libya in an effort to depose Muammar Qaddafi and his government. What if he couldn't get into the country? What if someone wasn't able to get him out? What if Jim was injured or even killed in one of these strikes?

The world is filled with What Ifs, What Ifs, What Ifs.

Jim went off to Libya.

———————

The thing I hadn't properly comprehended at the time— before and after the *Stars and Stripes* debacle—was that Jim was a freelance journalist. I knew the word *freelance*. Everyone does. Back then it sort of tripped off my tongue and toddled away. *Freelance*. I didn't attach any particular meaning to it—he was independent, working for himself. Most new young journalists begin as freelancers. But, unlike in decades past, there are fewer and fewer staff positions for them to gravitate towards. Jim was interested in a stable home for his writing, but more and more that home was located in the floating air, the ether of the internet.

Our earliest written evidence for the word "freelance" comes from Sir Walter Scott's *Ivanhoe*, in which a lord refers to his paid army of "free lances." It referred to medieval mercenaries who fought for whichever nation or person paid them the most. Scott writes: "A man of action will always find employment."

A freelancer is a writer who doesn't have a particular home base. They fly by the seat of their pants. They don't have insurance and—when they're not embedded—they have to find any form of protection that they can get for themselves. They have no security teams. Some of them can't afford the proper first aid and the hostile environment training that is so necessary. It is largely a life for the idealist. Freelance journalists see their mission as a vocation, not a job. For Jim, there was possibly even something faintly spiritual in it. It affirmed a faith he had in human nature. But this faith also meant that it was a sort of Franciscan venture: he did what he had to do in the world and there was not a whole lot of reward. No freelancer gets paid a lot. I was shocked to learn that Jim was only getting $70 for some of his articles. His stories would sometimes take weeks to investigate and write, so that essentially amounted to pennies per hour. He didn't care. He was living a life that he felt destined to live. It was where he felt most acutely alive.

Freelancers have to risk themselves. They never know if their story is ever going to get published. They stay in the scruffiest hotels. They drink in the darkest bars too, almost inevitably in the corner, a group of them, their ashtrays full, their glasses clinking. They share secrets. They have to barter with security guards and fixers. They need to find the right translators. A flak jacket and a helmet are crucial to their uniform. Most freelancers would like the steady salary and protection offered by the big news outlets—BBC, NBC, Al Jazeera—but a part of them likes the maverick side of things too. They are independent sometimes to a fault, and they are extraordinarily loyal to one another. They may want to be first to the story, but they also want to be first to the rescue of a fellow journalist if his or her situation goes awry.

And so Jim arrived in Libya as a freelancer. He had already undergone two in-depth safety training courses. He was carrying a satellite phone. He had tried to get medical insurance but couldn't find any company to cover him. He hired a local "fixer" as a translator and guide, then crossed the border from Egypt and found himself in a car on the way to Benghazi. What if. What if. What if.

The whole of Libya was—in Jim's language—an utter shitshow. A couple of weeks earlier, a multi-state NATO-led coalition began a military intervention in response to the civil war. They were trying to implement an immediate ceasefire including an end to some incredibly egregious attacks against civilians which amounted to crimes against humanity. There was a ban on all flights in the country's airspace. Sanctions had been tightened on the Qaddafi regime and its supporters. A naval blockade was in place. Tomahawk cruise missiles were slamming into strategic targets all over the country.

Most staff journalists from the major media outlets had withdrawn because of the increasing danger. A gaping hole in information grew. There was very little on any of the major news channels. The newspaper columns were largely empty. Silence. Which led to more violence. And consequently, even more silence. This gaping void drew more freelancers to cover the historic events. The freelancers—a motley crew of cynics and idealists if ever there was one—stayed at the Africa Hotel in Benghazi, the cheapest and worst hotel. Crumbling concrete. Bedbugs. Ceiling fans that shook. Jim's good friend and fellow photojournalist Nicole Tung described their situation as "journalism on a shoestring." That description was polite: it was more like journalism on a raggedy old thread.

During the day, they'd go out and record the impact of war and talk to civilians, protestors, anyone who might have something of interest to say. To the journalists who remained, it mostly seemed like a *Mad Max* war—there were rebels, and then there were government forces, and sometimes they were indecipherable. They all rode around in pick-up trucks with guns mounted on the back and flew their giant red, black and green flags from the top of their cabs. Over the hill they went, with their stereos blazing, as if there was a soundtrack to war. And then back over the hill they came with the handles of their guns too hot to touch.

Killings were indiscriminate. Torture too. Bombs went off downtown. In the evening—after writing their reports—

the freelancers gathered in the bar where the glasses on the shelves, and the shelves themselves, shook.

Freelancers usually scramble to find the best breaking story. So the hotel should have been a competitive environment. There's always that moment in the movies—a reporter gets slipped a note and she suddenly disappears through the kitchen, startling the chef, running out into the world. But the journalists who spent time with Jim in Libya later told me that he transcended competition. He just wanted the news to find a home.

In a way, Jim was feeling what soldiers surely feel when they are at war. The proximity of death gives everyone camaraderie at its finest. Share another cigarette. Investigate another source. Meet me in my room. Let me pay the restaurant bill.

He was writing and filming. There was no U.S. Army to tell him what he could or couldn't do anymore. He felt liberated. John and I saw him on CNN, PBS News Hour, and CBS Evening News.

He was speaking the language he was born to speak: an ongoing history that needed to be shared. As he said in a speech at Marquette University after his six-week captivity, he wanted something new, something fresh, something authentic: "I wanted to get ahead."

"Getting ahead" meant getting at a deeper truth. What Jim had noticed—and what he took to heart—was that there were families behind the front line who were suffering in profound ways. Men, women and children, whose lives depended on what was going on. He wasn't just reporting a political war. He wanted to report a human war too. But to report a human war you had to report the other war too.

Getting to the front line was the holy grail for journalists at the time.

Early on the morning of Tuesday, April 5, 2011—after he had been in the country a little more than two months—Jim and three other journalists, on a tip, caught a ride with some rebels along a coastal highway where a portion of the battle was happening. The tip was hot. There was a real chance that they would get some good footage. In the red minibus with him were Clare Gillis, an American reporter who had just graduated from Harvard; Manu Brabo, a Spanish photographer; and Anton Hammerl, a South African photojournalist.

"We were under the spell of the front lines," said Manu afterwards.

The rebels drove them out along the coast, close to Brega, an oil town, where the conflict was raging. Their driver was a teenage boy. They drove through checkpoint after checkpoint. They knew the front line was looming. The minibus stopped at a rise in the road. They could feel their guts begin to tighten. Two other pick-up trucks zoomed past them. Jim later wrote that the rebel convoys were like schools of fish hunting together with no clear leader or command structure.

Over a small hill, they saw some young men standing around a sedan. Jim and his fellow journalists leaped out of the minivan to do some quick interviews. Clare asked how far away Qaddafi's forces were and one boy said: "About 300 meters." That, they knew, was astoundingly close. A mortar or a rocket could easily have been dialed in within seconds.

As a group they decided that they should back off a little

and they moved to the side of the road into what they thought was relative safety. Not so.

"Two heavily armed Qaddafi pickup trucks came over that rise and fired," remembered Jim later in his reports. Manu said that he and Jim ran and ran and ran. They were laughing as they ran, not a funny *ha-ha* laughing, no, but a frightened, exhilarated laughing, a wild laughter, the sort of laughter you might get when you're both terrified and alive, in the throat of death.

They dove to the ground. Bullets whizzed above their heads. The sound of it to Jim, he said, was like machines eating metal.

They crawled their way along to find shelter under some small trees with Clare. The shooting intensified. The three of them were together now, but they couldn't find or see Anton. Jim crawled forward to a small sand dune with his camera still rolling. He spotted Anton crouched about ten meters ahead of him. The bullets whizzed over Jim's helmet. He realized that the soldiers were not just shooting indiscriminately but were shooting directly at them.

Ahead of them, Anton let out a weak cry: "Help." Jim shouted at him: "Are you okay, man, are you okay?" The voice grew weaker: "No." The bullets whizzed around. Shouting and screaming came from all angles. "Help me."

This was war and it was not pretty. Their friend and colleague had been shot, and they were unable to help.

Jim threw up his hands and shouted the Arabic word for journalist: *"Shafa! Shafa!"*

He, Clare, and Manu were rounded up at gunpoint by troops loyal to the Qaddafi government. Jim was severely beaten with the butt of an AK-47. They were thrown in the back of a truck by a group of young soldiers. Their hands were tied behind their backs and blood pooled in the back of the truck.

Their—and our—44-day hell had begun.

Anton's body was never found.

I was sitting with my mother at Margarita's, a Mexican restaurant in Dover, when my husband called. John had just heard from Human Rights Watch. "Jimmy has been captured by Qaddafi loyalists," he said.

These were the sort of moments when the world proved to be bizarre and brutal at the same time. One moment there's a plate of chips, a bowl of salsa, a couple of glasses of iced tea, a pleasant chat with a loved one, a favorite restaurant, and the next there's a gaping hole in your consciousness.

I sat there, trying to take it all in. I had heard the word "they" and felt strangely comforted that at least Jim wasn't alone.

Driving home, the chorus of questions rang in my head: How did it happen? Who was Jim with? Was he being tortured? Was he able to pray? Did he have enough to eat? Was he going to be all right?

For us, it was a dizzying introduction into the world of hostages and hostage-taking. We were advised by the State Department to stay quiet and let the diplomats work behind the scenes. Our son Michael took charge of the situation. He met with ambassadors and other officials in Washington, D.C. He reached out to a friend of a friend who was working for

John Kerry, chair of the Senate Foreign Relations Committee.

Still, the silence pounded. I prayed. John prayed. We spent hours in the nearby Adoration Chapel. It was the beginning of Lent so our daily scripture readings became foundational. I asked for strength to increase my faith that God was with Jim and the other hostages.

After a while, we decided to go public with the news. It was a risk that we felt we had to take. Jim didn't have a huge media organization behind him with a crew of attorneys making daily calls to the State Department as had a group of recently released *New York Times* reporters. But we did have our posse of friends and family. His childhood friend, Brian Oakes, created a webpage. His college pal, Tom Durkin, had T-shirts and buttons made. Another pal, Peter Pedraza, offered invaluable service with public relations. My brother-in-law Fernando put up a "Free Foley" Facebook page. Jim's Teach for America colleague Sarah Fang took on the social media accounts. We held candlelight prayer vigils. Phil Balboni, the president and CEO of *GlobalPost* became an integral part of our campaign. Other vigils were held around the country. Our neighbors in Rochester tied yellow ribbons around their trees. The Saint Charles Home, a local orphanage, was right around the corner from our house, and the children there were all praying for the hostages, as was our entire church community.

David Bradley, co-owner of *The Atlantic*, formed his own research team in Washington, D.C. to figure out ways to get the hostages out. The catalyst was Clare Gillis, who was a contributor to the magazine. We soon found out that David was one of the most kind, empathetic, honorable and distinguished human beings we would ever meet on this journey. We listened to him and took his wise counsel.

All of this was a huge learning curve for me. Before Jim's kidnapping, I was hardly able to figure out the remote for a TV channel. Now I was texting and tweeting and facebooking and whatever other technological "ing" existed at the time.

My life was becoming wired.

Jim and his fellow captors were now news. That's what we wanted. We needed to keep them in the public eye. We appealed directly to Qaddafi who had sons of his own, in the slim hope that he would respond to a father's plea. "As you love your own family without end, we love our own son and seek your gracious compassion in assisting him and the other three innocent journalists. Inshallah." I also wrote to President Chavez of Venezuela, a strong supporter of Qaddafi's. "We ask you as a father and leader who is impassioned about social justice and humanitarian issues to ask the Libyan government to release our son."

Neither replied.

Time crawled inside time. Was it possible the clock was going backwards?

I was alone in the kitchen on Holy Saturday before Easter, feeling very despondent. John had just left the house along with some of Jim's friends who had come to visit. I got out the silver candlesticks that Jim had brought home once from Jerusalem and started to polish them. That made me even sadder, and I started to cry, something I allowed myself to do only when I was alone. And then the phone rang.

"Ma, it's me, Jim!" Even to this day I can hardly remember what I said, but later Jim reconstructed it in his journal for the *GlobalPost*.

"Jimmy, where are you?"

"I'm still in Libya, mom. In prison. I'm sorry about this, so sorry."

"Don't be sorry, Jim. Oh, Dad just left. Oh. He so wants to talk to you. How are you, Jim, how are you?"

"I'm okay, I'm okay. I'm being well fed. I'm in with some Libyan prisoners now. They're giving me the best bed and I'm being treated like a guest. The others are okay, I think."

"Are they making you say these things—are they—?"

"No, the Libyans are beautiful people. They're treating me well, honestly. I've been praying for you to know that I'm okay. Haven't you felt my prayers?"

"Jimmy, so many people are praying for you here. All your friends have been calling, Donnie, Michael J, Dan, Suree, Tom, DJ, Sarah. And Michael is working so hard for your release. We love you so much! The Czech embassy is trying to see you and also Human Rights Watch. Have you seen them?"

"No," he said, and I thought I could hear the sound of someone in the background.

"They're having a prayer vigil for you at Marquette. Don't you feel our prayers?"

"I do, Mom, I feel them. But I have to go now. They're telling me I have to go. Mom, I'm strong, I'm okay, I should be home by Katie's graduation. I love you."

"We love you, Jim."

And then the line went dead. I stared at the receiver.

The conversation was a glimmer of hope. He was alive. He was convinced he would be home. Still the days stacked on top of one another, and no more phone calls came. We waited for a miracle.

Jim was held in a cell with Clare for a while. One day he heard a knocking on the wall in the cell next to him. He leaned down to an electrical socket and whispered through it. The man on the other side was an American, Richard Peters, a contractor from Idaho, a former Navy Seal who had been captured. Richard had a Bible in his cell.

"You've got to walk with the Lord in here, brother," Richard whispered. "Don't go back to the Lord with nothing to give."

And so they prayed.

Life demands stamina and perseverance. After extensive research by friends of Jim's from Marquette and Teach for America, alongside David Bradley's team, Jackie Frazier, an American woman, had been brought to our attention. She had worked as a business advisor to Saadi Qaddafi, the dictator's third son. She left Libya during the uprising but had remained friendly with Saadi and was willing to go to Libya to see what she could do. She arrived in Tripoli and, using her government contacts, she had an almost immediate effect. Clare was released from prison into the custody of none other than Saadi himself. She was taken to a five-star hotel in his armored SUV. But Jim was not released. Our fear was that he'd be kept in Libya as a bargaining chip for the beleaguered Qaddafi regime. Calls were coming in from the Turkish embassy and Hungarian diplomats, and Harold Koh, the U.S. State Department's legal advisor. Then came the rather surreal news that somebody else, Nigel Chandler, a British journalist, had been released after being mistaken for Jim. After this was discovered, Jim was finally released into house arrest, and he was brought to a sumptuous three-story villa in Tripoli with Clare and Manu. It was mind-boggling, but the whole period was otherworldly in the extreme.

Who can put logic upon war and hatred?

And then it became even harder to understand. We found out the address of the villa and were concerned about it being bombed. A U.S. official at the U.S. Bureau of Consular Affairs told us that none of the information was actionable, that the villa was inaccessible, and that there was nothing that could be done about it.

Nothing that could be done about it? Truth is stranger than fiction. They were still hostages. They were in a prison that wasn't a prison. The NATO planes were flying overhead each evening. They heard the bombs falling at the same time as nightly prayer. They had fruit baskets and access to Hollywood movies—including, Jim told us, the 1963 remake of *Cleopatra*—but they weren't allowed to go outdoors.

Saint Augustine said: "Miracles are not contrary to nature, but only contrary to what we know about nature."

They were finally released. Not only were the three of them free, but Nigel Chandler was too. They were taken before a judge who handed down a suspended one-year sentence. On May 18, the U.S. Hungarian protective power representative, Galli Laszio, pulled up at their guesthouse, and drove them across the city to the Rixos Hotel where most of the foreign press corps—their old friends—were staying. A Libyan spokesman, Moussa Ibrahim, welcomed them and—in an incredibly brazen act that almost defies understanding, except for the idea that everything in war defies understanding—stood up to say that they had been treated well, suggesting that their imprisonment had been routine, friendly even, and inviting the four of them to stay in Tripoli to continue reporting.

Two days later Jim and his brother Michael—who had worked tirelessly for this moment—took a long series of flights back to the U.S. in time for Katie's college graduation. Jim was elated to be home, or rather elated to be safe. But he was also pummeled by how the truth had been manipulated.

The Libyan spokesman hadn't said that Jim's friend and colleague—Anton Hammerl—was dead, and his body was never found. Jim was coming home from the front line of death and disinformation.

When he got home, he said: "The first thing you lose in war is the truth."

Moral courage. These were the words that fired up his eyes when he came home. That was the essence of what he spoke about when he was invited to universities on speaking engagements. He had bored in on his own personal truth. It may sound a little high-minded to some, but he had earned it. The two words together mean so much. *Moral. Courage.* To be principled in the matter of right and wrong, and to manifest high principles for proper conduct.

Jim never mentioned the principle directly to us, but we saw it in him—and in many ways we found a new Jim—by watching his speeches on video after he returned home from Libya. There he was, in front of college audiences, fiercely defending what he believed in. It was a new idea to me, but it has since become a foundation stone. I like the way these two words meld with one another and, to me, they bring out the essence of Jim. His courage was moral. His morality had courage.

There was so much gratitude on Jim's part when he arrived home. He knew that he was incredibly indebted to so many people who had played a role in bringing him to safety. His brothers, of course. His friends from college. Phil Balboni. David Bradley. Jackie Frazier. Dozens of anonymous people who had taken to Jim and to the plight of other journalists. It humbled him. The phone calls came in. Letters too. He even went with me to a local convent where the nuns had been praying for him. Sister Mary Rose handed him a scapular of Our Lady of Mount Carmel. He grinned, put it on and said he wouldn't take it off.

While there was gratitude, there was darkness too. He stayed in touch with Anton's grieving widow, Penny, in the hopes that Anton's remains might be found. He wrote for the *GlobalPost:* "I couldn't sleep. And sometimes I didn't want to. I didn't want to be alone with my thoughts. It took me a month to come to terms with the guilt I felt over the decisions we made that led to Anton being shot that day."

He was really disturbed to learn about how hard his disappearance had been on his family and friends. He watched the tributes to him from a vigil at Marquette and got the "weird feeling of going to your own funeral."

We suggested counseling, but he said he was fine. He put his head down and started writing thank-you notes. He spent the next month visiting all those who had helped. He plowed his heart and soul into communicating with fellow freelancers, inquiring about other hostages he had met while in captivity. And he organized a Christie's auction in New York to raise funds for the children of Anton Hammerl. The inability to save Anton continued to hit him hard. He carried it with him. The guilt ate at him. It was a war wound. I'm not sure he ever recovered from it.

"Foreheads of men have bled where no wounds were," is a quote he wrote in one of his notebooks from Wilfred Owen, an English poet, one hundred years earlier.

That summer he moved in with his brother Michael and his family outside Boston. *GlobalPost* CEO Phil Balboni gave Jim an editorial desk job. But Jim was restless. Michael's wife, Kristie, told us: "It was like Jim had an itch he couldn't scratch while he was domesticated." Phil joked about taking Jim's passport away. After staying up to play with his nephews, he would get straight to work. He tried to get used to sitting behind a desk, but he still had the taste for being out in the field. He wanted action. More than that, he wanted to speak up on the part of those who did not always have a voice. I'm sure he felt himself to be a conduit. It was something he found to be humbling and compelling. The unknown was a good place for him to be.

Jim also said: "When you see something really violent, it does a strange thing to you. It doesn't always repel you. Sometimes it draws you closer. Feeling that you survived something. It's a strange sort of force that you are drawn back to."

There was a promise in the Arab Spring, even if, in some places, that promise was already being torn asunder. It was a movement that Jim thought was emergent—far greater than the sum of its parts. It might look naïve in hindsight, but at the time there was a genuine and fervent hope that the Middle East, in particular, and the world, in general, might be able to propel itself into a new landscape of democracy.

By the fall of 2011 he was back in the Middle East working with Human Rights Watch. He was able to move around quite freely. With Clare, he returned to Libya to the place where his fellow journalist Anton had been killed. They stood in the desert, at the bend in the road, and remembered their colleague. Anton had been the victim of a war crime. They could not find his body, but they paid him homage. He was one of more than 11,000 people missing in Libya.

Jim flew back home in May for a fundraiser for Anton Hammerl's children. But then he was away again.

By the time he floated the idea of going to Syria to us and his friends, it sounded like he had already made up his mind. He admitted to his close friend Tom Durkin that Syria was more dangerous than Libya. Tom was stunned. Jim was set. His jaw was clenched.

I know I did not do enough to stop him. The intensity of his desire to tell the stories overwhelmed my increasing concern. But I also knew I wouldn't have been able to stop him. *Hold your tongue. Watch your loved one go.* This is the language of so many of us: mothers of soldiers, husbands of doctors, wives of activists, children too.

He was last home in the United States for his 39th birthday on October 18th, when we celebrated with his favorite Spanish paella, and then he was off again, thrust in the middle of the world of conflict, saying that he would be back by Christmas.

Several of his friends argued with him not to return to the Middle East. John and I added our concerns for his safety, but he was committed to returning. He had found his vocation. "Mom," he said, "I have promises to keep."

Jim wrote prolifically in Syria throughout 2012. He spent a week covering a Syrian hospital to report what was happening there. He wanted to inspire his readers to reflect on what really happens in a war. People get hurt. Children lose limbs. Hospital lights go out. Death is in the air. After observing the abject misery in the wards and the operating theaters in Aleppo's Dar-al-Shifa, Jim began to raise money to buy an ambulance. Clare Gillis warned him against the project, noting that militant groups could co-opt the ambulance to trick civilians. But, as Clare later remembered, "Jim thought about the best-case scenario, not what could go wrong." If the hospital needed an ambulance, he had to try to get it one. And he did.

The longer he worked in the conflict zone, the quieter he became. He was less and less attached to what he owned. When we asked him what he wanted for his birthday, he said that he wanted a pair of tough pants with lots of pockets, something that wouldn't rip or stain. He already had his flak jacket, but he was thinking of himself further into the combat zone.

On one of his last nights in town, his brother Mark took him to a comedy club in Boston. Jim, who normally enjoyed a good laugh, sat stone-faced. He left early. But they hugged. And they remembered that hug: it would become a poignant memory for Mark.

Jim wanted to live in the present. And the present to him was happening elsewhere.

He was determined to bear witness to the horrific bombings and gassings of innocent civilians by the Assad regime. He wanted to cover parts of Syria where most other journalists feared to step. In a *Newsweek* article he wrote: "The idea was to go past where the majority could go, get better stuff because no one else was there." It was his idea to "go in sooner, stay longer, go closer."

The last time I ever spoke to Jim was in mid-November 2012. I was between patients at our family practice clinic. I picked up the phone and told him that I was sorry but I couldn't really chat. He said: "That's okay, Mom," and he went on to offer condolences for my 104-year-old aunt who had died a few days earlier. There was Jim, always thinking of someone else.

"I'll call you on Thanksgiving," he said.

I never heard his voice again.

The Voice I Hear

It is difficult for me to piece it together. It comes in fragments and random images. They are in a taxi. They are forced off the road. Blindfolded and zip-tied. Bundled in the back of another car. The radio plays loudly. They dare not even whisper. The car drives fast. The potholes are severe. For him, everything now is about listening. Sometimes the radio reception blanks out and he thinks that they have entered a garage or they're travelling under a highway overpass. He vows to count the times the radio blanks out: perhaps, then, he can find a way back. His captors scream and call them traitors, spies. He hears them mention the CIA. He tries whatever Arabic he can. *We are journalists. We mean no harm. We're not CIA.* The car halts at a checkpoint. They are bundled out. Punched in the back of the head. Made to run. Forced into another vehicle. Punched again. They are told to keep their heads down. They come to a stop. The doors open. They are hurried along. They are pushed down a set of steps. The sound of clanking doors and keys. A room. A cold floor. Silence.

I try to reach for him, but he is too far away. The images will not stop coming. I try to block them, but they return. Even in my sleep, they return. He is so far away and yet he is here. He tries to stay calm. He tries to breathe slowly. He prays. Silently.

Okay, Ma, look away. Don't watch. Go back to sleep. Don't watch this.

I was concerned when we did not get a call from Jim on Thanksgiving 2012. He faithfully called on holidays and family birthdays, even when stationed far from home. The day slipped away, as Thanksgiving days do. The sky darkened. The leftovers were put away. The board games were boxed. We dimmed the kitchen lights and crawled off to bed. We slept, fitfully. Surely Jim had just forgotten? Lost track of time?

The sun rose. We checked our computers. Nothing. No news was good news, I said to myself. Then, as we sipped our morning coffee, the landline rang—it was Clare Gillis, calling from Turkey. Alongside Nicole Tung, she was calling to tell us that Jim was missing again. He had been travelling with John Cantlie, a British journalist, just inside the Syrian border. The two, it turned out, had been taken and whisked away. Their trusted translator and fixer, Moustafa, had been set free.

The news came as a chest-thumping shock. I stood rooted to the spot. Deep down we all knew that something like this was possible again. Not that we anticipated it, but we feared it.

I stared at the phone. The thing was a curse.

The news upset his brother Michael greatly. Michael had pleaded with Jim not to return to Syria, and he had taken a lot of time off from his work in order to ensure Jim's safe release. Still, he reluctantly took the lead once again in gathering whatever information we could find. I knew it was a strain on him and his young family. I admired his courage. The rest of our family chipped in wherever we could. We were familiar with the system from the first kidnapping. We had done this before. But Jim's captivity in Syria was nothing compared to his time in Libya. "It's going to be 45 to 100 days of hell and then we'll have him back," Michael said. In Libya we had a good idea within a few days where and by whom Jim was being held, and we had some eyewitnesses, but this time around, in Syria, we couldn't figure out anything at all.

Our first point of contact was the FBI. Within a week of Jim's disappearance, an agent came to our home in Rochester. He was kind and polite, but it shocked me that he seemed totally unprepared for the assignment. When he asked if we had considered asking President Assad for assistance, I thought he must have been joking. Were we going to lift the phone and ask for our old pal, Basshar?

The agent did not speak Arabic, nor had he ever been to Turkey or Syria. He did not even ask for Jim's cell phone number. Three weeks later, this same FBI agent was on the Turkish border trying to make sense of the rumors and many conflicting leads to Jim's whereabouts. He was as lost as anyone else.

Jim had vanished without a trace. We had no idea who had taken him. We were aware that Syria was a quagmire of competing factions: government loyalists, gangs, rebels, splinter groups and Al Qaeda. There were rumors of a group called ISIS and a variety of other Islamic loyalists. The acronyms were an alphabet soup. It felt as if we were spinning in several different directions, all of them out of control.

The FBI urged us not to tell anyone that our son was missing, assuring us it would be better for Jim. I wasn't sure how silence could help, but I wanted to believe that Jim would be found and brought home soon. I tried to remain calm, but inside I was overcome with terror and horrific anxiety. My chest felt inordinately tight. I found it hard to breathe at times.

Our lives paused in Jim's absence. In December, when our daughter Katie became engaged, she refused to set her wedding date because she wanted to wait for Jim's return. So, on one hand, we were desperately trying to find help to find Jim, to free him, and then on the other, I wanted to continue helping our only daughter plan her wedding. Terror on one side, joy on the other.

The days fell like dominoes. We obediently went through Christmas, telling no one but close family. By the New Year, we had heard nothing new from the FBI. The agent assigned to us seldom called, and the few times he did, it was to gather information from us, never to offer any.

Five weeks. Six weeks. Seven.

Jim had left no instructions, no last wishes, no clues to his passwords to access his bank account or phone bills. We had to stop the automatic payment for his cell phone and end his newspaper and magazine subscriptions, but we lacked power of attorney. Phone call after phone call. Answering machines. Interminable waiting times. *We apologize for the delay—your call will be answered as soon as possible. We apologize for the delay—your call will be answered as soon as possible. We apologize for the delay— your call will be answered as soon as possible.* Imagine trying to explain to a salesperson at Verizon Wireless that your 39-year-old son no longer needs his phone, that you want to suspend his account temporarily, but you are unsure until when. When they ask why, you are not allowed to tell them. When they ask for how long it should be suspended, you have no idea. It was a daunting task, a small death in itself, one in a series of traumas. Ultimately, I found lawyers who offered their legal expertise *pro bono* so we could obtain power of attorney.

Still the days tumbled.

In January 2013, after two months of capture, we decided to approach the media and go public with the news. We went out into the snow and held a press conference at the end of our driveway to request help from fellow journalists in locating Jim. The *GlobalPost* convinced their insurance company to offer a security team to help. This generous gesture helped open several doors for us, but we still felt on our own in many ways. We briefly considered hiring a private security team but could not afford the $4,000 daily fee. An FBI supervisor, Donald Voiret—generally the only one to tell us anything—called to tell us that Jim was most likely being held at a hospital in Aleppo, but the *GlobalPost* security team disagreed. They thought he had been captured by Assad and taken to Damascus. David Bradley of the *Atlantic* graciously offered his help again and we accepted.

Still, we spun and spun and spun in place. It was hard to know what to believe. Was Jim in Damascus? Was he in Aleppo? Was he being held by the Assad forces? Worst of all: was he even alive? We heard nothing. Rumors came and rumors went. Competing information, lies, whispers. Several fraudulent calls offered us information if we would wire money. I learned more and more about the complexities of hostage-taking in a war zone, and what they called the K&R business: kidnap and ransom. Insurance firms. Security details. Experts in the field.

Some days would send up bright balloons of hope. Other days would deflate everything around us. Eventually it all bled into months.

Phil Balboni had graciously offered to use the *Global Post's* Kidnap and Ransom insurance to pay for a security company to help find Jim and bring him home. However, the security team worked for the *GlobalPost*, not our family. They had a trusted relationship with my son, Michael, but were unsure how to deal with me. Some of the team were reluctant to allow me in their weekly meetings. I was, I'm sure, the *emotional mother*, the *impulsive* mother. And perhaps there were times I was emotional and impulsive, but perhaps there was prejudice on their side too. Mostly it was middle-aged men who saw me as the 65-year-old mother who needed to be tolerated. Or rather they didn't see me at all. I felt invisible in the room. That was something I knew that I—and others of my generation—needed to fight against. We are so much more than one thing. We needed our voice in every room.

Most of all I had to believe Jim was alive. All the time, the questions rattled around in my head, some urgent, some quotidian, even banal. What sort of place was he being kept? What sort of food did they give him? Had he lost weight? Who did he have for company? Was he on a cold stone floor? What was he praying for? Was there light in the cell? Did he have anything to write on? Was he able to take notes? Did they give him medical care? To whom was he talking? Had he made any attempts to escape? Was he being moved from place to place? What way did the sunlight come into the room? Why was there such silence? Why could nobody locate him? Why was it taking so long?

The questions, even the simplest ones, took on an urgency that was difficult to bear. Thank God I didn't know about the torture he was going through at that stage. The possibility stalked our discussions, but it was never a fact. We were mercifully unaware.

At times I recalled the words of the hymn "Be Not Afraid," which was sung at church throughout Jim's childhood. I was just hoping he would remember that God was with him and the others.

At the same time life had to go on. In the summer of 2013 we held an engagement party for Katie, although she insisted on holding off her wedding until Jim returned home. And still there was no word.

How was it possible for any of us to find any solace?

My solace has always come in God. I am no theologian. I'm certainly no great thinker. But at some point you have to believe that the inadequacies of the words you use will be transcended by the faith with which you use them.

Prayer, for me, is the bread of the soul.

In the fall of 2013, we had a breakthrough. We received word from two strangers that Jim was alive. The first of these strangers, Dimitri Bontinck, a Belgian, excitedly reached out via Skype to inform us that his 19-year-old son Jejoen had seen Jim in a prison in Aleppo in northern Syria. Jejoen had been radicalized and went to Syria to fight against Bashar al-Assad's regime, but he was subsequently imprisoned by ISIS, then arrested upon his return home to Belgium. He had actually spent time in a cell with Jim and knew very specific things about him: his mannerisms, his tattoo, the names of family members. That made my heart soar. He was alive, he was alive, he was alive.

And then there was Omar Alkhani, who had accompanied the young American, Kayla Mueller, Jim's fellow hostage, into Syria. He reported hearing Jim's name and voice while in prison.

These two men had very detailed information to share with the FBI and our security team about where Jim was being held: a prison in Aleppo, once a former eye hospital. They knew the shape of the rooms, the length of the corridors, how to get in and out. They painted it in extraordinary detail: ten large cells, four meters by eight, a basement, iron-wrought gates. However, since Jejoen was held in a Belgian jail, and since Omar was difficult to contact, it took more than a month for the FBI to find and question them. By then Jim and the other hostages had most likely been moved. It was a missed opportunity. It landed heavily on my heart.

Then, at the end of November 2013, just over a year since Jim's abduction, our son Michael received the first email from Jim's captors. The wall was breached. In lower case letters it read: *hello. we have james. we want to negotiate for him. he is safe: he is our friend and we do not want to hurt him. we want money fast.*

The FBI told us that we needed proof of life questions in order to know if it was actually real.

"Proof of life." Such an odd notion. How does one prove that they are alive? Michael thought of three cryptic questions to which only Jim would know the answers.

Who was the goalkeeper of your high school soccer team?
Who cried at your younger brother Mark's wedding?
Who died when you were eight years old?

I tried to imagine Jim, in his dark cell somewhere, shivering, huddled under a blanket, his mind tripping back through a tangle of memories. I later found out from other hostages that this was one of his happiest moments while in captivity: "My family knows I'm alive now!" he shouted to Marc Marginedas when he got back to his cell, his hands raised above his head in joy. He told Daniel Rye Otteson that it was the best day of his life. "He and John (Cantlie) danced around like they just won the big lottery," said Daniel later.

When the proof of life answers came back to us via email, I felt a whole new bolt of hope move through me. My son knew that we were looking for him. There was light now. A crack in the doorway.

A new round of emails came. The kidnappers demanded the release of all Muslim prisoners and 100,000,000 Euros (one hundred and thirty million dollars). In fact, the demand itself was impossible to unravel properly—most likely they weren't just talking about Jim, but about the five other American and British captives too. Who was to know? The few encrypted emails we got were hard enough to untangle. We were back in the quagmire. The FBI told us to stall for time by telling the truth: we had no ability to meet the demands. They also said that they were unable to directly engage the captors on our behalf.

Life is priceless. But the actualities of life—too often surrounded by government and bureaucracy and war and greed and deception—is something else altogether.

It wasn't about money. There was simply no way that our government was going to get involved.

———————————

I loved my work as a nurse practitioner in our family medicine clinic but found it difficult to concentrate with Jim missing. I was more mother than nurse. I had to do something else, something concrete. Besides, the burden was weighing on the rest of the family. Everyone was exhausted. In the spring of 2013, I retired from my job. It was a big move. But I knew I had to do it. I had learned so much at this stage, and I did not want the burden falling on others. It was time to share the reins. Not everyone was happy with this, and I understand that: it was a big move. John was hesitant, and some of the children thought I was putting too much of a burden on myself. But I saw it as a way to unburden them, particularly Michael who had shouldered so much. They needed to live their lives too.

John and I felt that our silence had allowed the FBI and other authorities off the hook. Whether consciously or not, we had enabled secrecy and, therefore, a sort of inertia. We hadn't been pushy enough. There was a reason various officials did not want us talking about the kidnappings—they said it was to keep the hostages safe and to not increase their value to the captors, but in many ways I began to feel that it was about keeping them, the authorities, safe. Cynical as it may sound, it rang true. The secrecy seemed to be more and more about them and their jobs than it was about the safety of our son. I found this deeply troubling and yet at the same time I understood the motivation—here I was, trying to balance my contradictory ideas again.

The administration was following policy, but the policy was flawed. We had to get the word out. We had to penetrate the silence.

I travelled at least monthly to either Washington D.C. or New York City in hopes of getting some movement or action, perhaps a senator to speak out, or inspire a military advisor to create a rescue plan, or a way to get the issue on the forefront of the American psyche.

At first, I didn't even know into which D.C. airport to fly. Renting a car was a disaster—I tried to navigate the unknown streets and had no clue where to park. I didn't mind travelling alone, but it might have been more effective with a savvy companion. (John was at home, working: we touched base every night by phone.) But there I was, standing outside the Capitol—one of the most famous buildings in one of the most well-known cities in the world—in my soggy shoes and with my broken umbrella. Was I dressed appropriately? How could I figure out the hierarchy? How could I get past the gates?

Slowly I began to realize how doors could be opened. I sent letters. I left countless phone messages. If you worked hard enough, and politely enough, the door might open a crack. It took tenacity, stamina, desire, perseverance and prayer. I learned that the best way past the gate was not necessarily through the higher-ups, but through the assistants, the interns, the ones who were supposedly low on the totem pole. Treat them well and they might just reciprocate.

I visited with ambassadors, dignitaries, bureaucrats, politicians on all levels. I met with the Syrian ambassador, Bashar Ja'afari, twice. At the U.S. State Department and the United Nations, with the help of New Hampshire Senator Jeanne Shaheen, I begged for help. Time and again the reply came hard and fast: *The U.S. will not pay ransoms. We will not negotiate. This is best way to protect American citizens in general.* I begged to differ. Turning your back will not change the direction of the knife. I reminded anyone who would listen that Jim was still missing. Other countries had successfully negotiated for their citizens. They were not public about it. They worked behind the scenes. Why couldn't we do the same?

But I was not a professional hostage advocate. Many people helped—including former FBI agent Chuck Regini, Phil Balboni, David Bradley, Pete Pedraza and April Goble, a girlfriend of Jim's—but still, in the end, I felt very much alone. I had to scour the internet for the most economical ways to travel, the cheapest places to stay. No one ever mentioned submitting receipts for reimbursement of the thousands of dollars we were spending. Nor did anyone say that the government actually did have funds to reimburse for such travel and lodging. When I eventually found out, I was too embarrassed and disorganized to submit my receipts.

I struggled to organize all the meetings. Some faces were familiar, but others continually changed. I was received twice at the White House by Susan Rice, whom I had met when she was our U.N. ambassador. She was cordial and empathetic. She leaned across the desk, repeating the refrain that "Jim is our highest priority." At one stage she suggested that perhaps we could do a prisoner swap with those in Guantanamo Bay, but she quickly caught herself and referred me back to the FBI and the U.S. State Department. I soon felt like I was going in circles with no one taking real responsibility. Everyone said they wanted to help, but very few went beyond the platitudes. An FBI social worker called on occasion, offering some solace but nothing very concrete.

Another year ticked over, and the ball dropped on 2014. Jim had been in captivity for more than fourteen months.

Early in the new year the *Atlantic's* David Bradley called to make me aware of three other Americans who were being held with Jim. David was, and is, an extraordinary person, a big-hearted visionary. He contacted each family—the Sotloffs, the Kassigs and the Muellers—and we planned to get together in D.C. in April. He generously paid for all our flights and accommodations. He brought us together in the Willard Hotel, along with Nancy Curtis whose son, Theo Padnos, had also been kidnapped. John came along. We felt solidarity with the other parents. We met each other with mingled feelings of grief and optimism. We looked into each other's eyes and saw ourselves. We hadn't gotten anywhere alone, so we hoped we would be stronger together.

We finally got a joint meeting at the White House with a number of important people from our national security bureaus, including Lisa Monaco, Jen Easterly, Mark Mitchell, and Jake Sullivan, all of whom were sympathetic. But we later met with a large group from the FBI, where Mark Mitchell coldly told us for the first time that the U.S. would not do a rescue mission, nor would the government pay ransom, nor ask another country to help get them out. We became more and more aware that we were largely on our own.

Still, David Bradley continued to bring us together. He hosted the families for several weekends at his home. He was a friend and a mentor, a wellspring of emotional support. It is no cliché to say that the world is full of good people. We are bound and held together by a thousand small acts of kindness. Otherwise, we would fall apart.

Before we knew it, another Memorial Day ironically rolled by. Followed by an equally ironic Independence Day.

All the holidays seemed to mock us.

In September 2013, I was invited to do the Spiritual Exercises of Saint Ignatius. For 30 days over 30 weeks, a Catholic spiritual mentor guides you through meditations, prayers, and contemplative practices to deepen your relationship with God. I had tried these exercises many years before. When Jim was a toddler in Chicago, I brought him along to a meeting with the priest who glanced down at Jim and told me it was not the right time.

Now, almost four decades later, I felt it was the perfect time. I desperately needed to bolster my faith. I was ready for the spiritual direction the exercises could give me. They encouraged me to learn to sit quietly again. The lit candle reminded me of God's continual presence, challenging me to listen and be still with Him. I found a Mass app to use while I was traveling. I drew strength from being able to find a Catholic church wherever I went. It was good to know that I really was not alone. I tried to read the daily Bible readings. I prayed for strength. My faith sustained me, gave me courage and comfort.

It also allowed me to know that this world, as we experienced it, was not the endpoint.

———————————

I want to say it plainly. Spain paid to free its hostages. France did too. So did Italy. So did other nations. The United States and Britain did not.

It was not an official policy, but the European governments paid via an incredibly circuitous route, and one that is almost impossible to map. They insinuated themselves carefully into the communications system, got under the umbrella of the emails, and forged their own secret methods that included a network of agents and ambassadors and, yes, even spies. They used the cover of the families in order to communicate with the terrorists. Of course, the government itself never communicated directly. That was impossible. They wanted to have plausible deniability. Rather, they undertook a proxy operation. Information went through circuitous channels. Money was routed carefully through non-governmental organizations and intermediaries in far-flung places. It was very much cloak and dagger.

We were in Florida, trying to get a badly needed family break from reality, when we heard that the Spanish journalist Marc Marginedas had been freed. Then two other Spanish hostages were also freed. They were followed in March by four French journalists then, by the Italian Fred Motka. I was so happy for them; yet, I could not be happy at all. Why was our government doing nothing for the Americans?

Instead, we were threatened on three different occasions with criminal prosecution if we tried to raise ransom money for Jim's release and were clearly told that there would be no attempted rescue or negotiation through a third party. The absurdity of this was plain to me. The government wouldn't help us, and yet we also weren't allowed to help ourselves. Our pro-bono attorney said there was no precedent for such prosecution, but we definitely felt intimidated, nonetheless.

Meanwhile, elsewhere the ransom carousel was in full swing. It is estimated that some $40 million changed hands during 2013 for the return of the European hostages. It really did feel like the stuff of spy movies: signals from flashlights, cash in paper bags, motorbikes driven across the border, masked bag men held at gunpoint, clouds of dust around the receding taillights. Some of the hostages were given "goodbye" beatings. Others among them smuggled letters out.

Still, the British and American governments remained firm and ignored the negotiations by our allies: they stayed their course of promising and doing nothing. I was saddened and taken aback. How could the Spanish, the French, and the Italians negotiate and pay, while we were not allowed to *think* of paying, even privately, or through other conduits? But other families—including Daniel Rye Otteson's in Denmark—had managed to cobble together enough money, away from their governments, to get their loved ones home. *Why couldn't we?* was the mantra in my mind.

We knew there were ethical, political and policy issues at stake. We carefully weighed them all. We decided we would try. Let our government attempt to prosecute us. We called around and made great progress among our friends. A stranger, a friend of a friend in California, helped us put together a video about Jim. The Committee to Protect Journalists helped us find a videographer to film Joel Simon, their executive director, and David Rohde, a Pulitzer Prize winning journalist, talking about the need to protect those at the front line of truth. And we collected pledges of more than one million dollars. These were not donations, so we didn't have to deal with any physical money—rather, they were promises from trusted friends and acquaintances. Perhaps that would be enough. The going rate for a hostage, at that time, seemed to be between $2 million and $5 million. But what would happen if—as was not-so-subtly suggested—our donors were to be prosecuted?

I sent communications to the State Department asking for help and guidance, but I got no replies. Our government wanted to hold our hands and, at the same time, not go to the dance.

I began to think that one of our national tragedies is our failure to understand foreign conflicts. Too often we don't seek to know our enemy. Combine this with a paucity of empathetic engagement. Add in a reckless application of intelligence. All of it serves up a recipe for a nation that thinks it's doing the right thing, but it often seems to me that we're really just shooting ourselves in the foot.

It is impossible to learn something that you think you already know. That is America in a nutshell. We think we know, so we don't even try to learn.

The government continued what seemed to me to be a misguided obstinacy. And most crushing of all, we did not receive any further word from the captors. It was silence—

total silence—for another six months. It was time to find out how others had opened the doors.

In March, my brother-in-law, Fernando, and I got on a plane and met Marc Marginedas and his sister in Barcelona. They were wonderful. Marc was a well-known and well-respected journalist in his home country. He was bright and articulate and deeply empathetic. He had survived his captivity. That gave us hope. He told us everything he could about Jim and his situation. However, he was not able to divulge some of the information he had been given about the ransom or how the negotiations took place. (Still, years later, he is not allowed to tell me exactly how, and for how much, his release was secured.)

The Spanish government didn't talk with us directly. Nobody wanted to give away the "secret" of how they had managed to get their hostages—three in one year alone. We knew they had paid money, but the government officials would never say so, though in total it was probably in the range of $10 million. We were truly beginning to understand the complexities of ransom payments and the communications pipeline.

My brother-in-law had to return to the United States and I flew, alone, to Paris. It was not the Paris of candlelight and bakeries and strolls along the Seine—rather, it was one of taxis, the Metro and the cheapest hotels I could find. The French people I met were deeply hospitable, sympathetic, kind and polite. They were incredulous that I was there without U.S. government support. *What? You are here alone?* The Agence

France Presse, where Jim had freelanced, helped me with appointments. I met with the French journalist, Florence Aubenas, who had once been a hostage, and she introduced me to other families who talked about the media campaign to bring their four French captives home: Didier Francois, Nicholas Henin, Pierre Torres and Eduard Elias who had all been held captive with Jim. France, it seemed, was a different story than just about anywhere else. They cared deeply about their hostages. It was part of a national debate. Hostages would be shown on the TV almost every night. The names of captives were on the lips of schoolchildren. It amazed me. I was in awe, even a bit jealous, of this organized support.

I returned to gag orders and silence. We were left to our own devices. To this day it still raises the hackles on the back of my neck.

Through this series of meetings abroad we built up a picture of Jim's situation in Syria and what it would mean if we were allowed to negotiate. I refused to stop hoping. We had to dare to keep imagining a good outcome.

In June, Daniel was released and he immediately called us to share the message from Jim that he had memorized in captivity. It was astounding. He had learned it all, word for word, over the course of weeks.

I can still hear the sound of the determined crackle in Daniel's voice as he relayed it from memory over the phone:

Dear Family and Friends,

I remember going to the mall with Dad, a very long bike ride with Mom. I remember so many great family times that take me away from this prison. Dreams of family and friends take me away and happiness fills my heart.

I know you are thinking of me and praying for me. And I am so thankful. I feel you all especially when I pray. I pray for you to stay strong and to believe. I really feel I can touch you even in this darkness when I pray.

Eighteen of us have been held together in one cell, which has helped me. We have had each other to have endless long conversations about movies, trivia, sports. We have played games made up of scraps found in our cell. We have found ways to play checkers, Chess, and Risk, and have had tournaments of competition, spending some days preparing strategies for the next day's game or lecture. The games and teaching each other have helped the time pass. They have been a huge help. We repeat stories and laugh to break the tension.

I have had weak and strong days. We are so grateful when anyone is freed; but of course, yearn for our own freedom. We try to encourage each other and share strength. We are being fed better now and daily. We have tea, occasional coffee. I have regained most of my weight lost last year.

I think a lot about my brothers and sister. I remember playing Werewolf in the dark with Michael and so many other adventures. I think of chasing Mattie and T around the kitchen counter. It makes me happy to think of them. If there is any money left in my bank account, I want it to go to Michael and Matthew. I am so proud of you, Michael and thankful to you for happy childhood memories and to you and Kristie for happy adult ones.

And big John, how I enjoyed visiting you and Cress in Germany. Thank you for welcoming me. I think a lot about RoRo and try to imagine what Jack is like. I hope he has RoRo's personality!

And Mark... so proud of you too, Bro. I think of you on the West coast and hope you are doing some snowboarding and camping, I especially remember us going to the Comedy Club in Boston together and our big hug after. The special moments keep me hopeful.

Katie, so very proud of you. You are the strongest and best of us all!! I think of you working so hard, helping people as a nurse. I am so glad we texted just before I was captured. I pray I can come to your wedding.... now I am sounding like Grammy!!

Grammy, please take your medicine, take walks and keep dancing. I plan to take you out to Margarita's when I get home. Stay strong because I am going to need your help to reclaim my life.

Jim

The Present Disappears

You fear the worst. You live in limbo. You are surrounded by doubt. You find yourself thinking about your missing loved one virtually every waking minute of the day. Something bubbles up in your mind and you think of the way he or she used to drink so much coffee. The way they used to walk. The way they used to tap the steering wheel. The terror of it all is that you do not know if they can do any of those things anymore. Every move you make brings you back to the person who is gone. It is a form of awful nostalgia. Your cell phone is glued to your ear. Every time it rings it could be good news. Then again, as you key it alive, it could be bad news. You freeze. Your stomach turns on its emptiness. You're not sure whether to answer or not.

Hello?

Your voice is always an octave higher than in normal times. You're not sure if you should be relieved that it's only your mother, or whether you should be disappointed in her for not bringing you some good news. Maybe someone else is trying to get through and your line is now busy. Maybe you should put the phone down. All is confusion. Am I going mad? What day is it? What month is it? And yet you know exactly how many days it has been since his capture: one hundred and two, three hundred and fifty, four hundred and thirty-four, six hundred and thirty-five. Time is torn asunder. The past resounds. The future looms. Maybe the present tense is no longer present. Maybe there's no such thing as the present anymore. Or maybe it is a permanent present.

Your life is a seesaw of emotions. Your friends call and gently inquire, but they are careful not to upset you. They're too careful. Why don't they just ASK? And moments later, why DID they ask?

Your husband calls with some ordinary domestic question—*Do we need milk, honey?*—and suddenly you resent him for not thinking about the distant one, the missing one, the gone one. How is he holding up? Is he being mistreated? You think about how resilient he was as a child. How he fell from that wall when he was four years old—he got right up and continued running. You've never really seen him break— he was not a boy to easily cry. And now you want to cry on his behalf. But what's the use of crying when you still have a million things to do? You have to call the FBI. You have to book that flight to Washington, D.C. You have to do the copy edit on the editorial for the *New York Times*. You have to pay the credit card bill. You have to sign up for a mileage account. You have to. You have to. You have to.

And then you find yourself at the fridge and the one simple reality is that you have to open it up.

His face is there on the front panel, a picture of him smiling from Christmas two years ago, with two smiley-face magnets holding it in place. You want to reach out for him. Your hands hover. You feel guilty even opening the fridge door because it means his gaze is not upon you for a split second. Why did you go into all trouble a second time, son? Why did you risk it? Why didn't you just stay here? In this house? This city? This country? Was it too suburban? Was it not enough? You could have written here. You could have undertaken so many investigations. You could have been a voice for the American dispossessed.

You swerve and think: Can you swap me out? Can they take me in your place? Your father will go too. Please just let us take your place. No questions asked. Anything. Anything at all. Straight swap. Are you listening, Jim? We will gladly walk in there so that you can walk out.

And then you realize that you're standing in your kitchen, but you don't know how long you have been there. You feel a flush of shame heating your cheeks. The fridge is fully open. Who in their right mind leaves a fridge fully open? What is happening to you? What have you allowed to happen to yourself? What has become of your world? The light is flickering on the emptiness. You search the shelves. They are very full, but they are very empty too. And you think, *Yes honey, we need the milk, we really need the milk.*

The phone rings once more and you hurry into the living room to pick it up. *Hello?*

I learned many things that I did not want to learn. And yet

there was no use in burying my head in the sand.

Jim was one of eighteen Western prisoners who had been kidnapped by the violent jihadist group ISIS. The terrorists tried to disguise themselves as another faction, but it was increasingly apparent who they were, especially as the other hostages came home, bearing witness. ISIS was masterminded by Abu Bakr al-Baghdadi who named himself Caliph of the Islamic State. The central kidnapping group was made of three British jihadists who had been dubbed 'the Beatles' by the hostages themselves.

Thankfully I knew none of this while Jim was in captivity, but the Beatles were relentless and savage. (I learned the details later from the hostages who got out, and from the articles that were written about them, and, much later, from the trial of El Shafee Elsheikh.) They kept a tight rein on their detainees. They did not hold back on waterboarding, or suspending their captors from the ceiling by handcuffs, or using cables to beat the bottom of their feet. They dressed in black and wore balaclavas and gloves. They never revealed their faces. They spoke in harsh Cockney accents and were the worst of idealists: newly converted to Islam. As Britons, they hated Britain. They were ashamed of where they came from. Their obsessions included Guantanamo, Abu Ghraib, the war on Islam, and the American occupation of Iraq. They kept their prisoners barefoot in case they tried to escape. They pressed guns to their heads, put swords to their throats, performed mock executions to terrorize them. They'd use a crucifixion technique to parody the U.S. war on terror: a reconstruction of the torture at Abu Ghraib where a hooded man is made to stand with arms outstretched. There were no nails, no cross. But there were beatings, relentless beatings.

Starvation techniques were cruelly employed. And there was waterboarding.

It was suggested that the Beatles were angered at the fact that Jim and John Cantlie had converted to Islam—because of that, it narrowed their possible reasons for torture. By Islamic decree, there were strict, and strictly enforced rules, for allowing one Muslim to torture another. The point of torturing hostages was to humiliate them and reinforce their sense of powerlessness. They wanted to sow panic. And the message they wanted to send was not limited to the cell within which they held their prisoners—they wanted the world to experience panic as well.

"The Beatles" label stuck in the public imagination. I only found out later through one of the hostages, Marc Marginedas, that it wasn't just because of their British accents that they were called the Beatles, but also because they enjoyed *beating* people. They were indeed the *Beat*-les. There was also media confusion around whether there were three or four Beatles (in the end, there were three) and who was John, who was Ringo, who was George. To the hostages, John, for instance, was Alexanda Kotey. But to the media—who liked the jangly ring of "Jihadi John" the name was attributed to the leader, Emwazi, who was later killed in a drone strike. Jihadi Ringo—El Shafee Elsheikh—seemed to have a particularly visceral loathing for Jim that amounted to a psychopathic hatred: it was said that he wore a cheap aftershave as if to advertise himself coming along the dark corridors.

But Jim refused to be cowed. I don't just say this just as a mother—all the hostages who returned say that Jim had a streak of stoicism and optimism in him that was difficult to quench, even in the most trying times. So much of what I heard from the hostages who were eventually freed reinforced what I, and Jim's whole family, thought about him. The Spanish journalist Javier Espinosa told us that Jim endured his torture with an unprecedented stolidity. He was persistent. And persuasive. He was able to negotiate on behalf of the hostages. In the cells, when he was with others, he often sat near the door so he could talk with the guards even if it risked a new beating. He asked for new clothes, better food, appropriate medicine. He learned how to communicate with hostages in neighboring cells either by tapping on pipes or passing messages along on lines of thread. He was also apparently one of the best at moving his spirit outside what they called "the box."

He was moved at least five times in the first six months of his incarceration. Once he was in a garage with a skylight. Another time he was in a deep underground bunker. Another, he was in a converted eye hospital. Every time the guards got spooked, or if there was a territorial move, they were whisked away. Over the following months he had lengthier and lengthier stays in different prisons: the days just piled up. Some of the time he was alone, but mostly he was accompanied by others, sometimes up to twelve people in a cell.

Together they organized games of chess and checkers, improvising with leftover fruit pits. Tournaments were held. Jim was strategically minded, and he organized a game of Risk, the well-known board game centering around diplomacy and conquest. He had played a lot of Risk as a kid with his brothers. Together, the hostages set out the borders and the boundaries, moving the pebbles back and forth across the floor.

From time to time there were, apparently, fierce arguments

too. When your world is reduced to a single, dimly lit room, the tensions can run high, even if it's only a game that's on the line. Food was stolen and hoarded. Sometimes they taunted one another. But the real taunts came from the guards. They forced the prisoners to sing a parody of "Hotel California," changed to "Hotel Osama"—repeating over and over again the line: *You can never leave.* For further perverse entertainment, the captives were forced to physically fight with each other— what the Beatles called a "Royal Rumble." If they refused to participate, they would be beaten. In these mock fights the captives tried not to hurt each other. They tried to hang on.

One can also imagine the longing, the fleeting moments of generosity and goodness and even laughter against all the odds. They tried to replicate an old world and they did their level best to keep themselves sane in an insane environment. The hostages told each other stories and they related the plots of novels that they liked. They gave each other mini-lectures. Jim's were on American literature. He practiced his Spanish, a language he loved. There were lectures on sailing and football. Daniel, a former gymnast, taught calisthenics. They used buckets of water as makeshift weights. They gave each other massages. This sort of camaraderie might be easy to make fun of—but when you're a hostage it keeps you alive.

They were so hungry they ate banana peels. They shared precious cigarettes, raggedy blankets, slept close to one another for warmth. For Christmas they had nothing to give each other, so they sat around and said something nice about one another: anything to remind themselves that they were human. They organized a jailhouse version of Secret Santa, a tradition in the Foley household. Each prisoner gave another a gift fashioned out of the trash. Jim's secret partner gave him a circle made from the wax of a discarded candle to cushion his forehead when he bowed to pray on the cold stone floor. Imagine that. They didn't want Jim to sustain a prayer bruise.

There was a time when Jim was being moved from one prison to another and he was bundled into a pick-up truck with others. In the truck there was a pile of clothes and Jim being Jim—irreverent, goofy—stuck a pair of underwear on his head for a laugh that would sustain them all even if only for a short while. There was so much to sustain themselves against, and any moment of lightness counted.

Sometimes the bizarre happened. One day their guards came into the cell armed with snowballs from outside. (I had forgotten that Syria could be cold and mountainous, and that the terrain could be extremely rugged.) The snow was like a gift from a strange country. The outside came in. The guards invited everyone into a light-hearted fight. But the next day they executed a Syrian prisoner outside the same cell, forcing him to his knees, delivering a bullet to the back of his head. From snow to bullets: who could live with such psychological torture?

Jim made at least two attempts to escape. He picked the locks of his handcuffs with an improvised skeleton key, but that's as far as he got. Another time, he managed to get out of the cell, but his cellmate John did not, so Jim gave himself up and surrendered to a terrible beating.

Beatings were the Beatles' thing. Even hostages who were being released received "going-away" beatings, a reminder that they had to carry with them, a mental tattoo to wear in the years to come.

As far as the chance of release, the hostages knew a

significant difference existed between the European hostages and the others. The Europeans had a real chance that they would be bartered for, and a ransom would be paid. On the other hand, the Americans and the British had a fair idea that their only real chance was a prisoner swap, and those odds weren't good at all. It must have made things quite tense in the cell.

Still, to this day, I am amazed by the bravery and endurance of all the British and American hostages. There are no weighing scales for the pain they and their families endured. In particular I think of Kayla Mueller. She was not in a cell with Jim, and she endured some truly unimaginable things on her own. She went to Syria as an aid worker, as did Peter Kassig, Alan Henning and David Haines. To help people. To relieve their suffering. They did not come home, but their stories of bravery, kindness and decency live on. It is one of the things that can never be taken from them. It gives hope even in the face of hopelessness.

———————————

When Jim had been held captive in Libya, he began to pray with his fellow cellmates. He washed alongside them and they invited him to prayer, which he did five times a day. He did not know that—in their eyes—this meant that he had converted and that, in the eyes of many other believers, he had become a Muslim. He wondered if he was violating his belief in Jesus, but that was a question without an answer. Still, it was pure for him, it was authentic, and it operated on two planes: any prayer that he could say was enough. It was a form of faith.

Then, when he was captured again in Syria, his practice

deepened, and he took the name Abu Hamza. He recited the Quran with fellow prisoners and prayed at least five times a day. This was no ploy. I'm certain that he did this in an honest way.

Sure, many supposedly "converted" in order that they might receive better treatment from the guards. But I know in my heart of hearts that Jim did this truthfully. The ritual allowed him to pray and focused him on doing so. The five calls to prayer undoubtedly drew him closer to God, giving him strength and courage to endure. I can see him there, in the dark cell, his prayer mat on the ground, facing east, his head bowed, whispering his prayers, a shaft of light moving at his feet.

Some people might believe that his conversion was an absolute thing. They want him in a neat box, sealed off and delivered as either Christian or Islamic. He certainly practiced Islam, but does that mean that we must label him and make him only one thing, or limit the extent of his faith and belief? Jim was ever curious and experiential. He was not interested in arguments driven by one note. He liked for the world to be shaken up. He knew that you can't get close to the fires of suffering without getting burned in some way. There was no point in living if you weren't learning. I can see him being interested in better understanding Islam and the jihad of his captors.

I also firmly believe that any faith that he had at the end was completely and utterly bedrocked by the faith that he learned as a child and young man. The depth of his Catholicism was the thing that gave him access to understand so much more. His years as an altar boy were there when he was in the cell. His first Holy Communion and his Confirmation were embedded with him. So too his days in a Jesuit university. So too his sense of social justice. I prefer to think that his faith was continually filling him up.

When he prayed at night he prayed to the past, the present and the future.

———————————

Days piled into days. Airport lounges. Waiting rooms. Taxis. Traffic jams. I continued trying to find out what was going on. There was good news. There was bad news. And on we went, another lounge, another traffic jam.

I was due to fly back from Paris in July 2014, when John called to tell me that we had received an email from Jim's captors threatening to kill him. The demands now included a halt to the U.S. bombing in northern Iraq. If Obama didn't stop the bombing in Yazidi territory, Jim would be murdered, they said. I felt a deep despair for the Yazidis, but for me—in what I see now as an almost helpless sense of hanging on—there was also a lifeline in the simple fact that captors had at least been in touch. They had written. They had made demands.

Earlier in Jim's captivity, I said I would go to the Turkish-Syrian border to hold talks with whoever I could find, but I was strongly dissuaded by John and our family. They felt that I, too, could get kidnapped. In so many ways, I already was. My mind had been kidnapped. My heart had been kidnapped. My time too. Still, I felt that there was some hope on the horizon. Such is the logic of longing. We hang on to whatever thread we can find. We had raised pledges for almost one million dollars. Other pledges would surely come in. There was a light on the horizon.

I should have known better. The captors were not talking to the Foley family or the Muellers or the Sotloffs or the Kassigs. They were talking to our government. They were making a proxy statement with a taunt. They had probably already made their minds up that they would kill our children. They needed a propaganda coup, and they were about to strike. They needed a moment around which to structure that strike—the bombings in northern Iraq provided them with a perfect prerequisite.

I didn't know it back then, but there was an attempt to rescue the hostages in early July. Operation Graphite Arrow. An unspecified number of Black Hawk helicopters were backed by fighter jets and surveillance drones. The men and women were made up of U.S. Army Delta Force soldiers and Navy SEAL commandos. They dropped down into the Raqqa countryside and moved in the direction of al-Akershi to a house that the hostages had called "The Quarry." They cut off the road and fought their way into a training camp, exchanging fire with militants as they went. They kicked down the doors but found no hostages. Not one. They were forced to retreat. There was a news blackout on the operation. I only found out about it a couple of days after Jim's death, on the phone call with President Obama. Part of it still makes me shiver with admiration and thanks that others had put their lives on the line for our hostages. One U.S. helicopter pilot was seriously injured while two ISIS fighters were killed. Another part of me recalls an intelligence officer admitting to a *New Yorker* reporter that their intelligence was "a little bit stale." The reality was the operation failed because our government waited until all the other negotiations by foreign governments for their hostages were over and done. There is diplomacy, yes, and there is courtesy, and then there is foolishness.

Mostly I wish they had engaged the enemy through proper negotiation. Imagine if they had prioritized the return of the American hostages. Imagine the wasted cost and risk of that Delta Mission. Imagine if they had funneled that money down through different channels: aid work, debt forgiveness, pressure from non-governmental organizations. Imagine if they had used ransom as a lure to track down the captors. Imagine if the United States had organized a coalition of nations to negotiate. Imagine if they could have used their wits rather than trying brute force. There is a reason why the concepts *brute force* and *ignorance* are so often lumped together.

Back home, I was exhausted. I took refuge in the Adoration Chapel in Rochester. I knew I had to surrender Jim to God. That meant, for me, surrendering him to God's Holy Spirit—His will, not mine. I had failed. I had been unable to bring Jim home. His fate was totally beyond me. It was not in my hands anymore. His fate belonged to God. I don't expect everyone—or even anyone—to understand this, and I know from the outside it might seem like a form of acquiescence, or weakness, but I finally knew that I had to entrust Jim to God's plan, not my own. I went to the church late at night. I kneeled down. I repeated my known prayers. The beads in my hands felt comforting. I felt a solid sense of peace move through me. An enormity of clarity cut through the pain and exhaustion. Through the Holy Spirit I felt reassured that God would set Jim free.

That was one week before my son's execution.

Now—many years later—it is still nearly impossible for me to piece it all together. There were so many vectors flying through the air, all at once, intersecting and deflecting and smashing into one another. I have heard about it from so many angles that it has become a jigsaw in my mind. Alexanda Kotey says that he was in a small Syrian apartment, typing up Jim's final statement on a computer. He had already seen the face of death. His whole life was given over to revenge. Emwazi was formalizing a propaganda assault. He was sharpening his sword for the executions, outraged by the American bombs falling not far away. The third Beatle, Elsheikh, has said that he was nowhere near the prison, but time would suggest otherwise. Jim was in his stone-floored cell. John Cantlie was with him. So too were Steven Sotloff and Peter Kassig. Tension stung the air. Jim's head was shaved the night before. Now he was told to put on an orange jumpsuit. He would have whispered his prayers. Rolled up his prayer mat. Stood and waited. Nobody knew if it was another fake execution or not. Time ticked. I was most likely in the house in Rochester, but who knows where I really was: I might have been floating off in my dreams, or writing another email, or at the sink watching the birds in the garden. No matter what, John was at my side. No matter what.

Elsewhere, the world went on. FBI agents were still trying to figure out the hostage locations. Military officers were making plans. Yazidi women were waking up to desolation. Reporters in Aleppo were treading down the stairs in the early morning to go to their breakfast before heading off to the front lines.

The guards came into the cell and handcuffed Jim. They hooded him. He would have gone obediently. He wouldn't want to make a fuss. He would not want to make it worse for others.

They forced Steven to go along with him. John too. To watch. To suffer. There had been mock executions before. Perhaps this was just one of those occasions. He would have been led down the corridors. He would have set his jaw straight under the hood. The guards would have taunted him. He would not be seen to be weak. He would be thinking about his family. He would be sending light our way. He would whisper silent prayers. They would have taken him in a pick-up truck. Early morning. Out to the desert. They would have lined them up in the sand. Unhooded them all. The hostages would have blinked their eyes against the light. The camera was placed on a tripod. Sand and distance. A few birds up on the thermals. The sun climbing higher. Its slow arc across the sky. He would have been singled out and led across the sand. He would have said goodbye to Steven and John. He knew now. He just knew. He had accepted it. The world was evil. He had learned that. But that was no great revelation. The point was to go beyond that. The world consisted of others. Everyone needed eyes that were human enough to see this: the world was made of others. Beyond this place. Beyond these sands. Beyond this time.

And it was time. They would, he knew, have him read a vile message. They would try to taint his family with lies. He would read the words with a slight tremble but a fierce stare. He would say these rote words in order to protect Steven and John and Peter and many others. He would say them too for those who write other words down, in other places, other truths. He looked in the camera and read the statement aloud.

The only thing that he believed went on underneath the words. The real truth was already home.

We had two funerals for Jim.

The first was hastily put together a few weeks after his death in September. My system was in shock. At first, we weren't even sure if we could have a funeral without a body. When we found out we could, we had to pick out a headstone and find appropriate readings from Scripture. Our bishop in New Hampshire presided. This was the same bishop who had refused to do a Mass for Jim while he was in captivity—the living don't always get their proper due. But now—with Jim's death—the bishop insisted on it. I was not blind to the possible hypocrisy, but that was not the time or the place to take a stand.

It was a funeral without a coffin, but somehow—in the midst of all the grief—it turned into a celebration of togetherness, a true memorial. More than a thousand people came to the Mass. Boy scouts lined our streets with flags. The church was jam-packed. We truly came to realize what an impact Jim had had on the wider world. Father Dan, a dear local priest, sang the Prayer of Saint Francis. It was a beautiful outpouring of love and sympathy for our loss, a number of God's angels carrying me through the shock.

Then it was over, but it didn't feel over at all. There was a sense that there was so much still undone.

Jim's good friend, Brian Oakes, began filming a documentary about Jim's life, right there and then, at the funeral, almost as if he knew that Jim's story would belie his death. I was a little resentful about this at first and thought it might be intrusive, or become too painful to participate in, but

Jim: The James Foley Story would turn out to be tremendously important down through the years, finishing with an iconic song, "The Empty Chair," written and performed by Sting. The documentary and the song brought so many people together, akin to an answered prayer that countered some of the narratives that were out there.

I never watched the video of the beheading and I never will. The static image was more than enough. It had burned itself into my brain. There are so many times I wish I hadn't seen it, but the awful truth is that I did get a glimpse of him at the end, squinting in the sunlight to follow the script that had been written for him. But I knew that, even after he read aloud the words that others had written for him, Jim was speaking to his personal and absolute God.

He was not afraid.

Some of Jim's friends—especially those from abroad— had not been able to attend the first service, and many people asked if there would be another memorial. John and I genuinely wondered if anyone would return a second time, but they did—again, in the thousands. From Europe, from Syria, from Turkey and from all over the United States. We had a beautiful reception at Berwick Academy in nearby southern Maine with a slideshow where many poignant—and indeed funny—stories were told with friends from all his days: high school, college, teaching, journalism and beyond. Teachers. Editors. Mentors. The last of the freed Western hostages, Daniel Rye Otteson, was there too. So too was Jens Serup, the security expert. David Bradley. So many others. They all shared their love for Jim, his goodness, his empathy for others. They talked about his extraordinary ability to listen to others, alongside his strength to laugh at himself even in the midst of the darkest times.

Before we parted ways, we gathered outside in the dark as Jim's dear friend, April Goble, poignantly played *Amazing Grace* on her accordion. We held candles, and we held each other, and we cried.

A funeral is supposed to be where it all ends, especially if it's a second funeral. But for me it was a place to find a new beginning.

Seeing the World Anew

There are times I think of him in the narrow, noisy streets of Syria. Car horns. Radios playing. Taxis bouncing through potholes. A woman stands by a fruit stand, selling her wares. A young girl runs home from school wearing a pink neon backpack. An old man huddles around a game of *shesh besh* and pulls fiercely on his cigarette. A young man hovers in the corner by the alleyway, a sort of malevolence about him. He is talking politics and Allah and death. The air is ripe with bomb dust and the aftertaste of violence. There is the possibility of another attack coming. Everyone is listening, but not listening, for the whistle of a mortar through the air. Still, the market stalls open. The flower stall unfurls. A windscreen wiper pushes aside dust.

This is where Jim gets his inspiration. What he really would like to do is to walk through and not be noticed at all, become absorbed in the everyday. He would like his shadow to blend in. But he's tall. He carries a camera. He stands out.

Accompanied by his translator, he goes from stall to stall, house to house, corner to corner. He uses whatever he knows of the local Arabic. *Nice to meet you. What's your name? Do you have a moment to talk?*

More than anything, he wants to understand the ordinary person on the street. He desires the humility of getting to know another life. The foibles and the follies. The passions and the faults. Who is that woman and what sort of life does she lead, beyond the flapping tarpaulins of the small fruit stand? What does her home look like? Does she have a son at the front? Is there something she regrets not telling him? And what has that old man learned that makes his game of backgammon so important? How is it that he holds the cigarette so deftly between his teeth? How many stories does he tell between cigarettes? Where is that young girl going to, and what books are in her pink backpack? Where is her education taking her? And what about the young man in the sneakers and the white jeans, hovering on the corner, the sunglasses perched between his hair and forehead? What is he thinking? Is he on his way shortly to the front to fight? Or is he on his way to college? What occurs to him when the sunglasses fall?

Head down, eyes open, Jim walks among them.

I wanted more than anything to keep Jim's spirit alive. That was my challenge. I had spent the past few years plunged into a variety of worlds that I knew little or nothing about: kidnapping, ransom, terrorism, politics, bureaucracy.

Prior to Jim's kidnapping, the only time I had been in

Washington, D.C. was as a ten year old with the National Safety Patrol in 1958! It was hard to look back to that little girl standing in the crosswalk with her plaited hair and her bobby socks and her toothy smile.

Now my son was dead, and my optimism had been all but crushed.

But I didn't want to abandon that little girl either. She still represented something about possibility. I wasn't interested in closing off the past. Nor did I want to forget what I had learned over the past couple of years. Something fierce still burned in me. Some might call it anger, or disappointment, or determination, or any number of things, but I call it the Holy Spirit urging me onwards, giving me strength to harness a righteous indignation to help turn things around.

I was a 66-year-old woman. I missed nursing and that sense of healing, but somehow a different form of healing was making a demand on me. There was always the prospect of a quiet retreat into the garden, but I wasn't ready to give in yet. I did not want to disintegrate into the background. And I couldn't see myself idle. Besides, I had so much energy, much of it stemming from the outrage of his murder.

I had seen injustice all around. I had seen people's faith shattered. I had seen a government that had abandoned its citizens and left the survivors to pick up the pieces of the wreckage. Journalists treated like they were mere specks of dust. I had seen some of the cruelest things that human beings can do to one another. And yet behind all of that, I knew that a fierceness and a goodness still blazed in the world. I had also come across some extraordinarily generous and compassionate people. I had noticed chinks in the wall where the bureaucracy could be breached. I had heard—and admired—the notion that one could be an optimist even in the face of the worst reality. It seemed cowardly and wrong to remain in the darkness. Moving forward towards that light would take courage. Optimism is far more difficult than pessimism. Optimism lives outside itself. Pessimism simply feeds off itself.

Jim's notions of moral courage, along with the art of journalism, and the necessity for hostage return, had been bubbling in my mind for the past couple of years.

It was appalling to me that our government had no one responsible for the return of its citizens targeted abroad. There were no processes in place, no accountability. We had no single agency or office to help secure the return of Americans abducted abroad. There was a lot of talk but there weren't a whole lot of answers. There was the State Department, the FBI, our military, and twelve other intelligence agencies, but none of them really knew what the other was doing. We were drowning in disorder. Not only that, but we often underestimated the captors. They were clearly not the Junior Varsity team.

When it came to hostage situations, the U.S. supposedly had a non-negotiation, non-concession policy, but that was just another word for paralysis. We were wedded to policies, but not to our people.

And here I was, just weeks after my son's death, watching thousands of dollars pour into a nascent organization that we called *The James Foley Fund*. There was such a sense of outrage all about. People intuited a need for a change. They had seen a young man beheaded for the crime of being an American. And they were shocked to the core.

They reacted by sending us money. It wasn't meant to soothe us. I think the world was shocked by the stone-age brutality of ISIS. Intuitively, people knew that some deep sea change had to come about. They wanted to create something good. The *New York Times* and the *Boston Globe* each donated a full-page ad for the fund. After an appearance on Irish TV with Ryan Tubridy, money flowed in from Ireland. Friends of Jim's organized fundraisers. A permanent scholarship was established at Marquette University. There was a sense of global outrage, but also a feeling that things could change, and that the power lies with ordinary people.

But the awful news kept coming. The brutal murders of Steven Sotloff, Peter Kassig and David Haines. The rumors around the life and death of John Cantlie. The unconscionable rape and abuse of Kayla Mueller. The killings of Luke Somers and Warren Weinstein while in captivity. The alarm bells were sounding all around the world.

I confess that I can be emotional and impulsive. I can also be naïve at times. I drive forward, not always knowing how difficult it might be to reach my destination. A part of me thinks that I can just put my head down and go, and eventually I will get there, no matter what. But I had to face it—I had failed with Jim. I had taken over the reins for our family and I failed—abjectly, totally, utterly failed. I hadn't anticipated the depth of hatred of which some of the world was capable. I wasn't prepared for the run-around and the endless roundabouts of bureaucracy. I had swallowed our government's platitudes. My trust had bled over into naïveté. Jim's captivity was considered "collateral damage" by most of the government officials I met with. I felt that I hadn't lived up to the moral courage to which Jim had aspired. I hadn't spoken truth to power like he and his dead colleagues would have wanted. I had not recognized the power or the greed that operates on the fumes of fear.

I felt a visceral anger that I had been patronized, even lied to at times. I strongly resolved that our country could do better. This, I thought, could be Jim's enduring legacy. We needed to make the return of any kidnapped or unjustly detained American a national priority. Our U.S. hostage policy had to be improved to encourage the return of its citizens. Our government needed—at the very least—to be compassionate and transparent with our hostage families. A little honesty and understanding could go a long way. So much more had to be done to prevent hostage-taking. We needed to raise awareness. We also had to work on preventive security training, especially for aid workers and journalists, who were increasingly being targeted.

In other words, we needed to help cultivate a sense of national reckoning, both within our government and among our people. Our hostage policy in recent years was not just on life support—it had red-lined. And we needed a container—an organization—into which at least some of the solutions could fit. I wasn't quite sure what to do, but there were precedents, including a non-profit called Hostage UK that gave me early inspiration.

I suppose it's easy to say all this in the clarity of hindsight. At the time I was grasping for any way to keep Jim's sense of moral courage alive. Along with several other people— journalists, advocates, activists, friends—we wanted to try to change the nature of American hostage advocacy. Behind all the impetus and the fire and the fury, was my knowledge of what had happened to Jim and others. And behind that was my belief and my desire that things simply had to be transformed.

It is staggering now to think of all the people and resources that have come together, almost a decade after my son's death, to begin to put that change in place.

Hostage-taking is elemental. We care about the people we love. When they get taken, it digs a hole in our hearts. We want to fill that hole back in.

The practice of hostage-taking goes all way back to Biblical times, and probably long before that. Hostages were seized in ancient China and during the days of the Roman empire. In fact there's a history of Islamic groups holding American hostages since the 1780s when America went to war with the Barbary states. In more recent times we have had the Iran hostage crisis (1979), the Iranian embassy siege in London (1980), the kidnapping of Terry Anderson by Hezbollah militants (1985), Daniel Pearl (2002), Nick Berg and Margaret Hassan (2004) and many others. The idea of people being held hostage plays an important role in the American psyche, as it does everywhere around the world.

There are a lot of currencies in the world, but there are none as precious as a human being. And so the question of hostage recovery is one of the most profoundly contentious issues I know. Whenever and wherever human beings get together, there are going to be differences of opinion that shape who we are. The hostage debate is not just a matter of black and white. It inhabits several areas of complicated gray. And before you win—or lose—any argument, you must know the logic of those who oppose you.

On a simple level, a hostage is taken and a ransom is demanded. That ransom is negotiated until such time it becomes obvious that there is a final demand. The question then becomes should the ransom payment be made or not? It seems like a question that demands either a *yes* or a *no*. But soon so many other questions get thrown into the mix—not least the notion of trying to end the stand-off using force—and it becomes a hazy moral area. Still, the goal of the endgame is always the same—you want your loved one home, alive, unharmed.

The vast majority of kidnappings around the world are criminal in nature. Many, if not most, of these cases go unreported. In Mexico alone, pre-pandemic, there were a yearly average of 1,300 criminal kidnappings, but authorities concede that the real number is more likely ten to fifteen times higher. In America, however, kidnapping is a federal crime and—if reported—it lands on the desk of an FBI agent. Putting aside parental kidnapping and familial stand-offs, we don't have a whole lot of kidnapping in the United States, because we treat it as a very serious crime and are prepared to throw huge resources at it. This is not just a preventive measure. It's a sort of moral code. We do whatever we can to stop it from occurring, and if it occurs, we act.

The kidnappings of Americans that occur abroad have historically been treated very differently than domestic kidnapping. They fall under a very different bracket. They are generally perpetrated by militant and tribal groups, terrorists and even pirates. Sometimes states, like Iran, China and North Korea, have taken hostages or made arbitrary detentions for supposed crimes. It is estimated that there are about 250 or more kidnappings and wrongful detentions of Americans

abroad every year. That's five or six a week. The kidnappings
and detentions are undertaken for a variety of reasons—first
to make money, or to extract political concessions. Or they
can be perpetrated to sow a very real sense of fear in a people
perceived to be the enemy. And it's a very effective tactic when
it's carefully planned—unlike bombings or shootings, it can be
used as a basis for negotiation.

The most contentious area of all is whether or not we
should negotiate with, and possibly pay, the hostage-takers.
It's a tough question. A host of moral, strategic and political
questions come into play. There are also several emotional
issues at stake. We have all heard the *we-don't-talk-with-terrorists*
line. We have also heard arguments around public disclosure of
the kidnapping details. And we have also been privy to the idea
that if any money is exchanged it will be used to fund terrorism
and further kidnappings.

All of these arguments make sense, of course—and they
are, in their deep essence, true. But there is always so much
more than one truth. This is where the hazy area demands for
us to be more astute and agile in our deliberations.

After Jim's kidnapping, I began to know—not just to
believe, but to *know*—that there was so much work to be done
in this area. All around the world, people were being held
hostage for being American. If you held a blue passport, you
were a target. Why could we not have done more, and why
can't we do more in the future, to bring these innocent people
home? In this country we continually have the backs of our
servicemen and servicewomen in the military. "Leave none
behind" is the rallying cry for our armed forces. The idea of
forgetting them is appalling. Bringing them home is the right

thing to do. If a U.S. politician got kidnapped in the "line of duty" would we leave him or her behind? If a top-tier diplomat were whisked away by a hostile force, do we think we would just say a few words of hope and support and go on our merry way?

But what about the other brave citizens who dare to go out into the world as aid workers whose only mission is to bring compassion and comfort and food and life-saving information to the suffering? What about the doctors and nurses working without borders? What about the teachers who go into foreign territories to bring learning and nuance and awareness? What about the journalists who bear witness to history and the ground truth? What about the ambulance drivers in war zones? What about the clergy people and the contractors? The athletes wrongfully detained? Are they any less American? Are their contributions any less important? Is the idea that they "volunteer" for their duty enough for us to concede to abandoning them? Surely the good people in our armed forces and diplomatic services "volunteered" for their jobs too? We are, all of us, citizens. Our aid workers, our journalists, our teachers, our soldiers are no more or less patriotic than one another. Jim felt that he was doing his job as an American. He was bringing the reports of other people's suffering home so we could understand what was going on beyond our own shuttered windows.

I know that journalism has often been maligned in recent years. The idea of what is true and what is not true has been twisted. But what happens if no journalists are allowed to report on what is happening? What occurs if there is no accountability? What happens to the concept of truth itself? The truth is that the truth must come home. It must be borne by people we can count on to give it to us. This, in essence, helps to balance out other "truths." History is full of instances where the brave journalists (for example, those who wrote about the My Lai massacre in Vietnam) went against the grain of the government and illustrated the reality that saved countless numbers of lives. The existence of a free press is at the fundamental core of our democracy. But journalists are being imprisoned and detained all around the world on a daily basis. Why in the world would we abandon them?

It is true that ransom payments can be used to finance terror groups. It is one of the reasons why so many people—my family and I and the families of the other hostages included—paused to think about the morality of handing over money that might finance their cause. It was one of the Obama administration's favorite arguments: *If you pay a ransom, it encourages more kidnapping.* It's a solid argument, but it doesn't cover all the complexities of the situation. In fact, the simplicity inherent in that argument is potentially dangerous. The shapers of this argument neglect to mention that the global arms trade also finances terrorists. So too does the misappropriation of American aid: money that gets sent abroad often ends up in the wrong hands or in regimes (the Taliban, South Sudan, Yemen, Libya) that are ripe with corruption. So too, for that matter, does international drug trafficking—in the past in Colombia the terror groups almost universally funded themselves with drugs that were sold on American streets. These are all areas where poorly conceived U.S. policies play a prominent role that are not to our advantage as a nation. What, for example, about the sale of weapons to Saudi Arabia, a country known to have strong links to terrorism?

Of course, no government wants to, nor should they be seen, paying for its hostage citizens. That would be absurd. We'd be providing terrorists with an ATM. All the cash registers of the weaponized world would start ringing straight away.

But believe it or not, the U.S. government—if the kidnapping is done on home soil—will actually, through the FBI, help a family, or even a corporation, pay a ransom. "If you're kidnapped in the United States...the U.S. government will not only negotiate, it will provide the ransom," says Joel Simon in his book *We Want to Negotiate* (the title of which was actually taken from an email from Jim's captors). "There are ransom stashes in Federal Reserve banks around the country, up to $300,000. And the FBI calls this 'ransom as lure.' They pay the ransom, they free you, and it's very easy to track ransom payments, and they arrest you."

Simon points out that if a government doesn't want to be seen at the forefront of negotiations, then engagement can always be done by proxy methods and subtle diplomatic channels. If a government—like Spain, for instance, or France—wants to get its citizens home, it does so in a variety of ways. Some of this has to with talking, not directly, but through non-governmental organizations (NGOs) or through friendly governments that are smaller and more agile and willing to relay messages to shady areas. Sometimes personal channels are employed, and private citizens are enlisted into the negotiating process. (One reason Jim's Libyan captors released him was because an "ordinary" American citizen,

Jackie Frazier, intervened on his behalf.) And what often resolves hostage-taking is—no surprise—the ability to engage the captors through direct negotiation. It is a fact that talking often works. In the end, dialogue is one of the greatest weapons we have. The ability to patiently listen and shrewdly negotiate is crucial to almost every outcome. The limit of our language is the limit of our vision.

Historically the United States and Britain have been the countries whose citizens are most frequently taken hostage. While we have a no-concession policy, our people get taken in greater numbers than those from other countries do. Surely this is as profound a challenge as any to the wisdom and effectiveness of our "no concessions" policy—a policy once referred to as "masculine" by the Secretary of State, William P. Rogers.

Perhaps, Mr. Rogers, we might try a dose of femininity? Call it decency, or nuance, or insight if you want, but it might help bring some of our loved ones home. I don't see this as a radical rallying call. I see it simply as a down-home truth.

———————

In the November 2013 email we got from Jim's captors they had written: *hello. we have james. we want to negotiate for him. he is safe: he is our friend and we do not want to hurt him. we want money fast.* It is interesting to break down exactly what they are saying. *We want to negotiate for him. He is our friend.* I wonder what might have happened if we had been able to take that email seriously? What if the FBI had been allowed to use their expertise to negotiate directly with ISIS? What if the U.S. had led a coalition of allied nations to negotiate all the captives free? What if we had gone through different channels? Where might we be now? Would Jim be reporting from a different area of the world? Would he be home? These questions might smack of naïveté to some, but I would ask the doubters to ponder the eventual outcome.

I'm not suggesting that all ransoms should be paid. Far from it. The notion of putting a price on a life is anathema to me. But if one is to go ahead and pay a ransom, there are several issues that must be raised. First of all, the argument can be made that not paying the ransom puts innocent lives at stake. A tragic choice is at the heart of all this: Who gets to live and why? Second, ransoms actually do get paid. International corporations pay them. Insurance companies pay them. Families pay them. According to Joel Simon and other experts, if a plane is hijacked, the ransom—more often than not—gets paid, at least initially. After that payment, another operation (to locate the perpetrators and bring them to justice) is often put in place by authorities. These payments are largely kept quiet, but they are a fact of life. We cannot bury our heads in the sand and say that they don't exist. As Joel Simon says in his treatise, there is very little data to support the contention that not paying ransom actually reduces the risks of future kidnapping. He points out that kidnapping is largely a crime of opportunity rather than one of intricate plans. Third, ransom payments, if they occur, don't have to be seen as a "concession." Ransom can, as pointed out, also be used as a lure, a honeypot. Sometimes the bad guys make mistakes. They get careless. The money can be followed and identified by forensic accountants. It turns out that even Bitcoin can be tracked. So it seems, in certain situations, that a ransom payment can be used to its own strategic advantage.

Then there's the literal cost of dealing with hostage situations by not engaging at first in dialogue, then engaging with force. Just thinking about the money spent on the failed U.S. Army raid in Syria in 2014 is mind-boggling. And even beginning to contemplate the incredible amount of money spent on the judicial proceedings for their captors Alexanda Kotey and El Shafee Elsheikh—after the murders, after the fact—is enough to make your head spin.

All of this I have learned and mulled over as the years have unfolded. The truth, it turns out, is indeed multi-faceted. I don't claim to have the full answers. But I do know that the truth is muddied and that a clarity of thought can potentially reduce heartbreak. Researchers like Brian Jenkins of the Rand Corporation were often quoted by the administration, but his research actually showed the outcomes for U.S. captives was much worse than for hostages in other countries.

One of my essential questions has always been: Why did we get the Z-team—the essentially uncoordinated response—when Jim was first captured, and why did we get the A-team—the very best of American justice—after he was killed? Why did we spend so much time and money in the aftermath of his death and very little on the extension of his life? Why did we become laser-focused only after his beheading? Where do our priorities lie? How can we shape our national priorities so that the lives of our people are at least as important as our foreign policy and economy?

Of course, life can't be quantified in dollars, or even words. Think of it this way. Your phone rings. Your daughter has been taken. A ransom is demanded—let's say a million dollars. You put down the phone. Your hand is trembling. Who in their right mind doesn't immediately think: I need to get a million dollars?

It's the human way. We love each other, sometimes to death.

In November 2014, three months after Jim was killed, I had a meeting with President Obama at the White House. I was still upset with the president and his administration. I felt they had abandoned my son and the three other hostages. However, I was grateful to him for giving me his time and I wanted to be as respectful as possible.

I recall being ushered into the room and sitting alone with him at a long dark table. He was sipping a cup of tea. I was a little surprised that nothing was offered to me. Still, it wasn't a time to worry about manners. I found him somber and rather cold. The length of the table seemed to reflect a distant emotion. I got the sense that he didn't want to have the meeting, but it was probably a case of him responding to optics. It was likely that one of his staff members wanted him to take the meeting.

We exchanged pleasantries and then the president stunned me by saying: "Jim was my highest priority." I felt the oxygen disappear from the air.

"I beg your pardon, Sir," I replied. "He may have been a priority in your mind but not in your heart. Jim and the others were abandoned by our government until much, much too late."

The words hung there for a moment. The president didn't argue with me, just continued sipping his tea, his eyes downcast. I teared up a little and he rose up from his chair and handed me his white handkerchief. I was grateful for that momentary kinship, but then it was over, and the door was opened, but only for me to leave. It was very brief, less than ten minutes.

A few photos were taken of us and later sent to me. I didn't put them in a frame.

When Jim was captured, all the branches of our government were strictly told that they were not to communicate with the kidnappers. Yet, they wanted to shape our emails and our responses. We would like to think that "our guys" are smarter than the "bad guys," but in 2014 our policies were arbitrary and inconsistent. The FBI has extensive experience in negotiating with terrorists, but they were not allowed to intervene on Jim's behalf. What happened to us—with the government leaving our family to negotiate on our own, and literally threatening us with prosecution if we dared to raise a ransom—was shortsighted, heartless and arrogant.

Fair enough, we did listen to the FBI. We took their advice. But often they were singing from their tattered old hymn book. At times they were tortuously slow in responding to our emails. Often their suggestions about what to say to the kidnappers repeated *exactly* what other hostage families were told to say, word for precise word; therefore, the kidnappers knew they were not actually dealing with a family member, but with a proxy government official. There was no imagination, no sense of an individual life at stake. They were so buttoned down and buttoned up at the same time. I don't want to suggest that this was the fault of the agents themselves—rather it was the policies and the regulations that handcuffed them.

When I met with Susan Rice in January 2014, she proposed that there could be a prisoner exchange with Guantanamo for Jim, but she quickly did a turnaround and suggested that I go back again to the FBI. Then she implied that she was powerless to help. I began to detest that word, *powerless.* Especially when it came from such powerful people.

Five months later—and just a couple of months before Jim's death—it was extraordinarily difficult to watch the news of the Obama administration releasing five senior Taliban commanders held at Guantanamo Bay in exchange for the U.S. soldier Sgt. Bowe Bergdahl who had reportedly deserted his position and became a prisoner of war in Afghanistan. I was happy for the Bergdahl family. The prisoner swap was billed as a trust-building measure with the Taliban, but the Taliban was still considered, on many levels, to be a terrorist organization. The Taliban prisoners included two senior militant commanders who were said to be linked to operations that had killed American and allied troops, as well as being implicated in murdering thousands of Shiites in Afghanistan. The released men were flown from Cuba in the custody of officials from Qatar where they were given a one-year travel ban.

Imagine being a mother and seeing this news when your son or daughter is still in captivity. Imagine the surge of hope. Imagine, then, having to deal with the reality that it is not going to happen for you and your child.

A one-year travel ban? I'll take it, yes, please. Thank you so much for bringing my son back.

There are moments when the world turns itself inside out. Two months after he was killed, Jim's birthday rolled around. It was hard to think that he wasn't on the other end of a phone. John and I went out for an early dinner. It was a moment lined with sadness, but when we arrived back in our New Hampshire home at dusk, we saw 40 lighted candles spaced out over our front lawn. It took my breath away. Small acts of kindness, like small acts of mercy, can realign the world.

Donations and pledges continued to pour in. Within weeks of Jim's murder, Rachel Briggs of Hostage UK had visited to urge me to help fund the Hostage US start-up. The Foley Fund was able to secure, and match, a $250,000 grant from the Ford Foundation to help care for the private needs of hostages and their families, including their financial, legal, medical and psychiatric needs.

We changed our organization's name to the James W. Foley Legacy Foundation to stress his legacy and to open the path to the future. We decided our mission would be to advocate for freedom for Americans held hostage abroad and to promote safety for aspiring journalists. After Jim's murder, the doors of the White House suddenly opened to us. One of our first meetings was with Lisa Monaco, Jen Easterly and Susan Rice. Our middle son John Elliot accompanied me. We had a chance to vent our frustration with U.S. policy and we insisted the U.S. could do better to bring innocent Americans home. To be fair, they gave us the time of day, listening generously and closely.

We were finally beginning to be heard. In December—just over three months after Jim's death—President Obama ordered the National Counterterrorism Center (NCTC) to do a full review of hostage policy, which would include interviewing all affected families. This was conducted under the extraordinary leadership of Colonel Bennett Sacolick, a former Delta Force commander.

Present and former hostages, and their families, were invited to participate. Each was privately interviewed about their ordeal. It felt good to vent and to be listened to. We could perceive a possible chink in their refusal to change. Light was squeezing through. We could see it spread across the floor of doubt.

Very quickly—in fact, astoundingly—the hostage review became presidential policy. In June 2015 the "Hostage Recovery Activities" report was announced. President Obama invited all participating families to the White House and went on TV to explain it to the world. The directive formed the Hostage Recovery Fusion Cell, a Special Presidential Envoy for Hostage Affairs, and a Hostage Recovery Group at a National Security Council level. It stressed accountability as essential for deterrence.

Our government finally saw the necessity of operating in a proactive, coordinated manner to bring American hostages home. Jim's legacy, along with that of the other hostages, was beginning to reverberate. We had made a significant dent and we would continue to evaluate how well this new hostage enterprise was working. When Donald Trump was elected, we were shocked at his refusal to evaluate the previous administration's directive. We began our own Foley Foundation research. We confidentially interviewed former hostages and their families to evaluate the effectiveness of our new approach. The family of Robert Levinson—one of the longest-held hostages in American history, presumed dead in Iranian custody—advocated to make the Presidential Policy 30 law. It was suggested that criteria be added to include the determination of wrongful detention abroad. So it wasn't just about hostage-taking. It was about those who were wrongfully jailed, too. Our collective impact was deepening. The Robert A. Levinson Hostage Taking and Accountability Act passed through Congress in 2020, with support from both sides of the partisan divide. It turned out that President Trump was active in actually helping to bring our people home. He appointed an outstanding Special Presidential Envoy for Hostage Affairs, Robert O'Brien, to lead diplomatic efforts. Shrewd diplomacy, direct dialogue and the prioritization of our U.S. nationals held captive abroad proved incredibly effective. Some of it was done for the photo opportunity, with a political strategy in mind, but his administration did help bring several hostages back, among them Michael White, Sam Goodwin, Pastor Bryan Nerran, and Joshua and Thamara Holt. Some of it was done with a carrot, some with a stick, but at least it was done. More than 50 hostages were brought back from 22 different countries.

This melding of legislation and action across administrations seemed to be working. Within the supposedly impossible, the possible actually exists. The red and the blue can actually settle into a shade of purple.

Some significant steps were taken to protect journalists too in what has essentially become a worldwide assault on reporters. Leaders like Steven Coll, the dean of Columbia School of Journalism, brought many great writers together—including author Joel Simon and former hostage David Rohde—to meet at the U.S. State Department and at Columbia. Concerns about the abusive use of freelance journalists in conflict zones were aired. Eventually I became a founding member of another non-profit, A Culture of Safety Alliance, beginning with the development of safety principles for editors and freelancers to address the high risk that journalists, especially those in conflict zones, take. A graduate level journalist safety curriculum was written by Jim's former journalism professor, Ellen Shearer. It was supported by Reporters Without Borders, among others. Later we developed a series of undergraduate safety modules for journalists, written by Jim's dear friend, Tom Durkin.

The days came and went. The years did too. My 70th birthday rolled around, and the advocacy work went on. Some days were good, some days were bad. I was a family nurse practitioner with a lot still to learn about the world of hostage advocacy and journalism safety. I wondered sometimes what in the world I was doing. But there were other days when it felt as if the work was as necessary as breathing. Sometimes I wished for silence. I suppose everyone does. I wanted the world to be at peace and at ease. On occasion it felt as if I was spinning and spinning on the merry-go-round. I came full circle then full circle again. My family sustained me. They didn't always agree with what I was doing. At times I'm sure they felt a little neglected and irritated with the work. *You do too much, Mom,* is a refrain I know well. *You're travelling too much, honey. You've got too much on your plate.* I'm sure they were right, but I couldn't stop. There always seemed to be another American taken hostage, another desperate family to try to help, another job to fill, another interview request, another board meeting, another congresswoman to meet, another email from a reporter. There were so many facets to a non-profit that had me floundering.

But I was continually challenged by the memory of Jim and the desire to see his legacy flourish.

We organized the Foley Freedom Run, an annual five-kilometer run/walk. The Rochester Fair grounds were decorated with pumpkins and flowers. More than a thousand runners showed up to pound the pavement and display their support for press freedom and the freedom of those unjustly detained around the world. As the years went on it was amazing to see tens of thousands of people come together in groups all around the world: London, Paris, Madrid, Singapore. Even during Covid the event went ahead virtually.

We also initiated the Foley Freedom Awards in Washington, D.C., as a way to elevate the issue of hostage-taking, and to help families connect with one another, with the attendance of government officials and interested journalists. To bring people together. To heighten awareness. To salute some of the heroes who do the good work of changing the world. It's a formal event. I enjoy dressing up and thought it would be a good way to have fun and attract donors. John, on the other hand, is not so fond of the black tie. But like the whole family, he's a good sport. Always, they know, it comes back to Jim and his legacy.

With this in mind, I invited former President Obama to speak at our virtual Foley Freedom Awards, honoring Jim. He accepted and spoke directly, eloquently. Several former hostage families were angry that I asked him to speak since they felt that he had abandoned their loved ones. But I felt it was the right thing to do. I wanted to give the president a chance to repair what had happened all those years ago, and I was grateful for his time and his sincere empathy. He didn't have to record a speech for us, but he did. And he repeated my words from when I met him in 2014—America could do better, far better, to help bring our people home.

The message wasn't lost. In the spring of 2022, several families came together to launch a family-led "Bring Our Families Home" campaign. The group developed a black and yellow flag, similar to the Prisoner of War flag, to represent all people held as political prisoners and hostages, and to show solidarity between those who are gone and those who remain. They held a press conference in front of the White House and came onstage at the Foley Freedom Awards to light candles for their loved ones. How it pained me to see families continue to suffer what we had endured.

Towards the end of summer, President Joseph Biden gave an Executive Order on Bolstering Efforts to Bring Hostages and Wrongfully Detained U.S. Nationals Home. He declared that "hostage-taking and the wrongful detention of U.S. nationals abroad constitute an unusual and extraordinary threat to the national security, foreign policy and economy of the United States." It came under the umbrella of the National Emergencies Act.

The tide was starting to turn. The wrongful arrest of WMBA basketball star Britney Griner in Russia in early 2022 dramatically increased media interest in arbitrary detention and hostage taking. The flash bulbs lit up Russia this time. Paul Whelan had also been wrongfully detained by the Russian security services in 2018 and then given a ten-year sentence. The government and our media was tuning in more and more to the growing list of injustices. The tide continued to shift. In the fall of 2022, the Biden Administration ratcheted up its efforts, securing the release of seven American executives who had been wrongfully detained in Venezuela. Baquer Namazi, who had been unjustly held captive since 2015, was released from Iran.

By the time our 2023 Foley Freedom Awards rolled around, 27 U.S. nationals had been freed under the auspices of President Biden's office. They included Jeffrey Woodke, a Christian aid worker held six long years in Niger, and Paul Rusesbagina, the hero of *Hotel Rwanda*, wrongfully detained since 2020. In September 2023 the Biden administration also announced the return of five hostages, among them Siamak Namazi, Emad Sharghi and Morad Tabbaz, some of whom had been held in the notorious Evin prison for years.

Sometimes the world works, and a candle gives light to other candles.

———————————

There is still so much light left to be shone. The names of new hostages and wrongful detainees keep coming. In Syria, journalist Austin Tice was kidnapped in 2012. The psychotherapist Madj Kamalmaz, from Virginia, was captured in 2017. In China, Mark Swidan was unjustly arrested in 2012. Pastor David Lin, a naturalized U.S. citizen, has been incarcerated since 2006. An American Chinese businessman, Kai Li, has been detained since 2016. In the United Arab Emirates, American businessman Zack Shahin, designated "arbitrarily detained" by the United Nations, has spent fifteen years unjustly imprisoned. In Afghanistan, author Paul Overby disappeared in 2014, believed to be a prisoner of the Taliban. In 2020, in Venezuela, two former Green Berets,

Luke Denman and Airan Berry, were detained off the coast of Colombia. Eyvin Hernandez, a public defender from Los Angeles, was detained in 2022 and shipped off to a notorious Venezuelan prison. In two other high-profile cases, ex-Marine Paul Whelan was detained in Russia in 2018, and Wall Street Journal reporter Evan Gershkovich was held on charges of espionage, marking the first time an American journalist has been arrested of charges of spying in Russia since the Cold War. Educator Marc Fogel, arrested in Moscow in 2021 and charged with having medical marijuana in his possession, has not, at the time of writing, been designated "wrongfully detained." In Saudi Arabia, the names Dr. Walid Fitaihi, Aziza Al-Yousef, Salah Al-Haidar and Bader al-Ibrahim all evoke the injustice of the wrongfully detained. In Cuba there's Alina Lopez, a teacher. In Cambodia, the human rights attorney Theary Seng.

There are, in fact, so many more in so many other places. Cases that have long been held secret—in the hope of a breakthrough, or to keep the ransom price from being increased—keep surfacing in all corners of the world.

The names keep coming. They echo in my head, a sad and unjust litany.

The hostage enterprise structure is strengthening, but still not enough Americans are coming home. The average detention is five years. That's a long time away from home.

As I write there are over 50 publicly known American hostages held abroad. The word *public* is important since most families are told to keep quiet about international kidnapping in the hope of a quick resolution. There are many, many more, but their names and the actual numbers are classified. By the time you read this, some of these people will have been freed, some killed, others still imprisoned—staring at the same walls holding them in.

Jim once wrote on Facebook: "Everyone a story." And a story, he knew, is its own candle to light yet another.

In early 2018 Alexanda Kotey and El Shafee Elsheikh were captured in Syria while attempting to flee to Turkey. They were stripped of their British citizenship, and negotiations began to get them to America to face justice.

There were international objections to sending them to Guantanamo, and there were also objections to them being subject to the death penalty in the United States. From the beginning, John and I agreed. We were against capital punishment and a Guantanamo incarceration. We wanted our son's killers to be tried in a court of law and held accountable. The British held important evidence against them, but they could not release it unless the United States dropped the potential death penalty, which the Trump administration initially refused to do.

When these issues were resolved, the two were transferred from the Kurdish territories—where they were kept in tiny chicken-wire cells—to Iraq and ultimately the U.S. They arrived in Virginia on October 7, 2020, to face charges for kidnapping, torturing, starving six American and British citizens, and beheading five. They touched down in a land they hated. They sat in jail for almost a year, while the case against them was prepared.

Here were two men who had been involved in killing

my son and the other hostages in the most brutal way. But they were receiving the best of American justice—the court assigned them a strong team of lawyers and representatives to present their defense under the American law's presumption of innocence. They were to be fed and housed and given a chance to tell their side of the story.

They would be allowed to live—it had been agreed in advance that they should not be subject to the death penalty. They would get their day in court, and they would receive the dignity of justice.

In September 2021, John and I were present in the courtroom when Alexanda Kotey pled guilty to the charges laid out in front of him. He didn't glance our way. He didn't glance anyone's way. But part of his plea agreement was that he would talk with the victims' families. It took a while to decide whether or not I wanted to look this man in the eye, but in the end I knew that it was something that Jim would have wanted.

The following month I travelled to talk with Kotey. The prosecution team met me outside the Virginia courthouse in the rain. This was the A-team. They had prepared relentlessly for every possible outcome. They were extraordinarily solicitous and kind.

And so it was that I came to spend two days with a man whom I got to know by the name of Alexanda. We tiptoed around the notion of forgiveness, but he did not ask outright for it. I would have given it to him, without a doubt. But while approaching the notion of forgiveness, he did not reach for it entirely. I felt in my heart that much of what he was telling was not true—especially when he claimed only to have beaten Jim twice—but I also felt a profound sadness for him.

For the very first time since Jim died, I cried in public. I cried for a lot of reasons, not least for the young children who Alexanda left behind in Syria. His daughters were now living in a refugee camp, unable to get out. He showed me their photo. Their faces scorched themselves into my mind.

On the exact same day we met with Kotey, we heard that the other defendant, El Shafee Elsheikh, also from London, decided that he would not take a plea agreement. He wanted to fight the charges.

So, the story would go on. A trial would happen. The world would get a chance to hear exactly what had unfolded in that distant desert. Elsheikh—the second of the Beatles—was about to test the American system of justice.

So That We Might Know

April 2022
Alexandria, Virginia

I find it hard to recall the exact details of the trial. It took two and a half weeks, but I think I went through a lot of it in a personal fog. Yet I can recall certain things with great precision, like stepping into the wood-paneled elevator in the Virginia courthouse. The doors closed. The elevator rose. I felt as if I was sealed off from the rest of the world for just a few seconds. The buttons lit, one after the other. On the ninth floor I walked into the elegant courtroom with the high ceilings. An aura of justice dwelled there, as if something *true* was about to unfold in that court. But there was a simultaneous tension too. I sat in the middle pews. My husband John came for a few days and my son Michael came to testify, but I also felt that I belonged to a much wider family too, sitting amid the living hostages who came to tell their stories and the other parents who I had known for years. We hugged each morning. We sat close to each other. We could tell what was going on, even behind the Covid masks. Day after day we listened to the testimonies and sometimes it was so harrowing that there was nothing we could do but hold one another's hands and close our eyes.

Then, at the end of the day, we took the same wood-paneled elevator down, and there were times it felt that it was descending not by any mechanical means but by the weight of the pain we carried. There were a series of round stickers on the floors advising people to stand six feet apart. But the rules were there to be broken and we crowded closely together as if the need to get outside, into the fresh air, was overwhelming. Still there was always a silence and always a refusal to look anywhere but straight ahead. Some people sobbed audibly. Sometimes the only movement was the passing of small packets of tissues back and forth.

What we knew was that four remarkable young people had lost their lives, and one man—El Shafee Elsheikh from Britain—was on trial for killing them.

He had been given the constitutional right to a full, fair and speedy trial. It was, of course, a grand irony—the ISIS warrior, in his most desperate moment, embracing the American way. He, unlike Alexanda Kotey, whom I had talked to six months before, did not take a guilty plea but instead demanded this great orchestration of a trial: all the flights, all the cars, all the meals, all the hotels, all the lawyers, all the lawmakers, all the federal agents, all the guards, not to mention the four defense attorneys—four!—assigned to him for the past few months, and probably a counsellor too. Even conservatively the trial was estimated at tens of millions of dollars. Nobody will ever be able to pin the labyrinthian figure down, since it covers so many different areas of government and civilian life, but it was suggested to me by one senior official to be upwards of $50 million. (I immediately thought of how many things could have been done in the world of hostage advocacy with that amount of money.) All paid for by the American taxpayer. In the pursuit of proper justice.

Proper justice was something Elsheikh himself had never embraced, but now it was his demand. And he had brought us all together, from parts all over the world: thirty-five witnesses from nine different countries.

From the outside it appeared to be a watertight case for the prosecution. A stateless man, a former British citizen, on trial for crimes committed against Americans in Syria. Four counts of hostage-taking, four counts of conspiracy to murder. There was video evidence, testimony from men and women who have been tortured, accounts from FBI agents, Scotland Yard detectives, and digital forensic experts. The prosecution had worked tirelessly for over a year shaping the case. They had gone back and forth to Britain and Syria. They had found eyewitnesses who lived now in Denmark and France and Canada. They had covered every legal, logistical and political angle, and they had built their arguments along the lines of an exhaustive offense in chess.

Still, anything could happen. And that *anything* lurked at the back of my mind.

The problem—and the underlying tenet of justice—was that Elsheikh needed to be proven guilty. Because until then, under American law, he was innocent. What, I had to wonder, if there were a prosecutorial mistake? What might happen if the jury did not agree? What if a technicality set him free?

Such thoughts haunted me as the trial progressed—maybe not so much the possibility of his innocence, as our side's potential inability to prove his absolute guilt. Elsheihk's defense team—all highly regarded American lawyers—had created an argument that relied on a case of mistaken identity.

It disturbed me that these lawyers were working on his behalf, but at the same time I thought it was a great tribute to our system. Elsheihk was getting a chance at justice, something everyone in the world deserved, and not everyone—as we, the parents of the dead hostages, well knew—got. His attorneys made the opening contention that there were more than 800 ISIS fighters who travelled from Britain in the years Elsheikh went there, and the prosecution had focused in on just three of them, nicknamed "the Beatles." They did not contend Elsheikh's presence in Syria. Far from it—he was indeed, they admitted, an ISIS fighter. But that didn't mean, they claimed, that Elsheikh was one of the Beatles. These men were, after all, always masked. They were identified only by their South London accents. They were variously called John, Ringo and George, but the names were regularly mixed and interchanged by the hostages and later by the media. They wore gloves. And balaclavas. They left no DNA. Any identification was a general one. Nothing could be specific. The eight counts—four of hostage-taking, four of conspiracy to murder—could apply to anyone with a British accent who had fought for the Islamic State. Elsheikh may have been in Syria, but there could be reasonable doubt as to whether he was one of the Beatles.

The thought of him going free lurked at the back of my mind like a small block of ice, slowly releasing its melt. Reasonable doubt. Reasonable doubt.

I didn't like him. I know that is a strange thing to say—how could anyone like their son's killer? But I mean it more in the sense of understanding him in the way that I had tried to understand Kotey a few months beforehand. There was something deeply malevolent about Elsheikh's presence. He was in his early 30s. He was slim and slight and quietly brazen. He had cut his black hair short and slicked it back with some sort of oil. His beard was hidden with a Covid mask. He wore preppy eyeglasses and western-style clothes designed, no doubt, to make him look more sympathetic to the jury—mustard-colored pants and a slim blue shirt, suggesting some sort of bizarre ISIS springtime.

Every day he entered the courtroom with his hands in his pockets and he sat with a slightly scornful lean, a short distance between him and his defense lawyers. I could sense the arrogance rolling off him. He wore no shackles, no jumpsuit, no sign of incarceration. He did not lower his head when the witnesses testified. Nor was he animated—no shake of his head, no shrug of his shoulders, nothing. He looked like the sort of young man who thought he has never met anyone better than himself. He showed no emotion that I noticed. We had been told that he was far more ideological than Kotey, but apart from the scraggle of beard there were no outward signs of his faith.

What would we possibly do if he were allowed to go free? We had to rely on the strength of the prosecution and the wisdom of the twelve members of the jury, knowing that sometimes it's such a slim margin between truth and terror.

Every day the other families and I trudged out into the Virginia sunlight, carrying the weight of the testimony we had heard. It was tough for all of us. But we needed to hear it. We had to bear witness. It was what our children would have wanted us to do. We knew about the beatings and the psychological violence and the starvation techniques, but there were certain details that were revealed that made the whole courtroom gasp. It was as if we shivered in unison.

Then there was the weight of the rest of the world around us too, pressing in from outside the confines of the Virginia courthouse. There were lives to carry on, relatives to take care of, businesses to run, decisions to make. There were health problems—two of the parents had to be taken to the hospital during the trial, one for a heart condition, the other for a dangerously bleeding nose. There were marital difficulties, and disagreements among the family members about whether or not we should talk to the media.

As for me, my only sister Rita in Houston was gravely ill with a severe exacerbation of her autoimmune disease. I also had a foundation to run. And my ailing mother to worry about. And grandchildren to look after. I was feeling scattered, and yet at the same time I was intensely focused on the court proceedings. We all wanted it to be over and done. We recognized that the end could lead, finally, to some sense of healing.

Watching the trial was unbearable at times. The revelations kept coming. Even after all these years, there was so much that I did not know about the beatings and the terrible psychological torture. Sometimes I didn't want to hear it at all. The words rushed over me and through me. But I stayed and I listened.

Every day, before a new round of testimony, I let my eyes fall upon a new scripture, and I prayed for the health and welfare of all around us.

One young man—I never found out who he was—carried a copy of Tolstoy's *War and Peace* into the courtroom and sat near the back. In the court's downtime, he read the book. He had cut it in half in order it to make it easier to carry. Some days, War. Some days, Peace.

I was sure that the trial was going to be a national sensation. I had expected the courtroom to be packed. There were even arrangements, in the beginning, for an overflow room. But as the days went on, I was surprised to see only a small scattering of reporters. Most of them were British, a couple of them French, but there were very few Americans. After the first day there was no *New York Times*, no Fox News, no *Washington Post*. That confounded me. After all, the trial was centered around four American citizens, two of them journalists, two of them aid workers. Why the silence? Why the absence? Was it shame? Covid? General indifference? Was it pure shallowness? I was deeply grateful for the journalists who were there, but what about all those who weren't? I have always thought that the most effective way to destroy people was to deny them a chance to speak, but why in the world would American journalists ignore a story that was fundamental not only to democracy, but to their very own craft?

When I opened the newspapers in the mornings, or strode across the hotel lobby and glanced up at the screens, mostly all I saw was Johnny Depp's face—his and Amber Heard's court case was taking place just a few miles down the road in Washington, D.C. I don't want to discount Depp's and Heard's case; however, I didn't want the lives of four young Americans, and a potentially historic case, to take a backseat to it.

The murdered hostages' story was one that the country needed to know. It wasn't just about Kayla or Peter or Steven or Jim. It travelled to the heart of American justice. Something profound was happening in front of our eyes. An international terrorist was being brought to justice in our homeland. They weren't being shipped off to Guantanamo or put on a leash in Abu Ghraib. Quite the opposite, in fact. The trial of El Shafee Elsheikh was the system at its finest, most dignified and most equitable: a jury trial rather than a bullet. So much that had happened in the Middle East had become a stain on our American soul and here, now, was a chance for redemption.

But the American cameras stayed away, apart from one young lady from CBS. Most of the major American papers only showed up at the beginning and end.

I felt a sense of shame run through me. Shame for my beloved country. Sometimes I just had to acknowledge the bland indifference that was apparent here, the inability to remember, the miniscule attention span, the disregard of history, the craven nod towards celebrity, not to mention the arrogance that we display to others around the world and our willful failure to understand foreign conflicts. But I suppose if we couldn't understand ourselves at home, how could we understand others abroad? We needed a sense of national reckoning, a proper soul-searching.

But, still, what eventually ran true—and what eventually

won out—was the incredible tenacity of the human spirit evident in the trial proceedings.

What happened in that courtroom will forever remain imprinted on my soul. I listened to the testimonies of my fellow parents. Their stories of their children felt all the more powerful in the high, echoing chambers of that paneled room. Jim had spent his last days with some remarkable people. It was important for me to remember that. It gave me solace. So much of the world is poisoned with narrowness, especially when it comes to war. But these four Americans operated on the flipside of war. Often, we forget that the supposedly anonymous are the ones who form the true glue of the world. Letters were read out. ("Only in your absence have I come to realize your place in my life," Kayla Mueller had written to her parents. "My heart longs to be with you all."). Photographs were shown. Tributes were paid. Former hostages came from Spain, France, Denmark, Iraq, and they told the harrowing truth about torture, waterboarding, starvation, abuse. Some hostages who didn't have to testify came anyway, simply to bear witness. It was amazing. They stared down their torturer as he sat impassively.

Experts contributed to the case, which was building word upon word, like stone upon stone, into a house of truth. Video technicians and voice experts were all involved. And all the while, the parents were present. Many of them were nurses and teachers and librarians. They formed the backbone of our country. They had raised their children well. Our children had gone to another part of the world in order to witness and help others. It was important that they not be forgotten. Or allowed to go unseen.

At one stage—in a moment that must be unique in U.S. judicial history—the judge, the Honorable T. S. Ellis III, charming and cantankerous in equal measure, was moved to tears by the speech of Steven Sotloff's father, Art. The judge buried his face in a white tissue so that the jury would not see him cry. I heard later that it was the first time in 35 years on the bench that Judge Ellis had displayed such emotion.

It was then that it struck me that much of our job—as parents—is to make the unseen visible, and to point to the importance of that which seems sometimes unremarkable.

When my day to testify came, I was nervous. But I had talked through the process with Prosecutor Dennis Fitzpatrick. He had guided me through what was technically needed. I had to identify Jim in a couple of family photographs and point to the fact that he was an American national. It was still early in the trial, and this was a matter of laying down bedrock facts. Still, I shook when my name was called. *Do you solemnly swear that the testimony you are about to give in this case shall be the truth, the whole truth, so help you, God?*

I took the witness stand and glanced down at the man who was responsible for killing my son, sitting no more than eight feet away. He was looking in my direction, but not looking at me. It was as if he were in some other space. He wore a mask behind the literal mask. His glasses didn't obscure his eyes which were deep and brown, but showed no light.

Questions for me came from the prosecution. I identified Jim in the family photos. I was asked why Jim had gone to Syria. "Jim went to shine a light on the suffering of the Syrian people," I said, "so that we might know what was going on there." I watched a video of John and me as we gave a press conference in our front yard, six weeks after the kidnapping.

I was asked if the remains of my son had ever been found.

"No," I answered.

It was a short, sharp interchange, brief and formal. There was so much more I wanted to say, but I trusted the prosecutors—they had their strategy.

But then moments later it was Michael's turn on the stand. This made my heart truly skip. The Foley men are often taciturn. They don't like to show emotion especially in public. They like to be alone with their pain.

He stepped up to the witness box and for fifteen minutes he answered questions primarily about Jim's identity, the emails we had received, and the communications we had with the terrorists. They discussed the use of the word "whilst" as an unusual and very British word that was often repeated in the communications. They also discussed the word "transgression," which was also used in communications.

And then came the moment I would never forget. Michael was asked to look at a photograph. The photo was not shown to the rest of the courtroom, just to the jury and the court officers. From the gallery I could not see it. But I knew what it was—oh, I certainly knew what it was.

A hush circled the courtroom. Not a single person shifted. The judge leaned forward in his black gown, his hands knitted.

"That's Jim," Michael said, staring straight ahead. "He's dead. The severed head is on his body."

A surge went through me: I will not call it pride or relief or sadness or anger or even each of these things melded together.

In fact, I do not know what to call it. But I knew it had taken an immense bravery for my son to sit in front of his brother's killer, and to hold himself together. I knew quite well that Michael would have loved to be able to step down from the witness box and deliver another form of justice to Elsheikh.

But he had done something far deeper, far more courageous. He sat in the witness stand. He took an oath. And he spoke.

That's Jim. He's dead. The severed head is on his body.

When Jim was twelve years old, he went to Spain with my sister Rita and her husband Fernando. Rita was his godmother, and they shared a very close bond. Jim went to Madrid to help with his young cousins—Joseph who was five years old at the time, and Maria who was just two. Often our paths begin to get carved out at a young age. Jim was only gone a month, but it seemed to bolster his interest in other cultures and travel.

One particular incident still reverberates in my mind, though I don't even know the exact details. Jim was able to save his five-year-old cousin who got in trouble in a local swimming pool. He didn't think of it as any great heroics, but the rest of us did: he had saved Rita's child from drowning.

Over the years he became closer and closer to his godmother, and Spanish became a language that he cherished.

But then it happened. Three-quarters of the way through the Elsheikh trial, I heard that my sister Rita's health had taken an even more dangerous turn. She was being moved to the intensive care unit in her hospital in Houston. I immediately booked a plane ticket to leave the next day. She had struggled heroically with her health over the years, battling her whole life against various manifestations of her severe autoimmune disease and she had never complained.

In the early morning hours before my flight, Fernando called to say that Rita had died. I had waited too long.

I suppose we all risk drowning at some stage or other— sometimes it's in our causes, and sometimes it's in our love, and sometimes it's in both. It is true that I always take on too much and it certainly seemed as if the waves were washing over me. The family had to be gathered. My 95-year-old mother needed words of consolation. There were services to arrange and extended relatives to contact. And then there were the memories to inhabit. I adored my sister, and it struck me that I hadn't appreciated Rita as much as I should have. Often we don't recognize the gifts that surround us. Rita had struggled. But she did so majestically and with great empathy. Things had come easier for me. As a child, I had always enjoyed school and friends. Rita had a stutter. She found it harder to fit in. But as life evolved, she had more than made up for any difficulties. She earned a master's in education and became fluent in French and Spanish. She was a talented and dedicated ESL teacher to immigrants in Houston. She was also a woman of great faith. Rita was a light in the world. She gave flame to others.

Now it was me stuttering. But I also felt Rita's spirit move through me.

After the service it was important for me to go back to Virginia to represent Jim: that's what his godmother would have wanted. I knew that the defense was just about to rest without bringing Elsheikh to the stand. The closing arguments were due soon. I had missed five days of testimony and then I got a message—as I was boarding my flight in Texas to come back to Virginia—that the closing arguments had come and gone, and a verdict was due in a couple of hours.

One part of the mother in me—the private mother—was ready just to go home and to be with my grandchildren. Another part—the public mother—knew that there was only one place that I could go.

This was Jim's story. And he was still telling it.

———————

I was exhausted. Yet another flight, yet another taxi. Pulling out from Reagan Airport into the scrum of traffic, I keyed my phone alive. Dozens of new messages. John. Katie. Michael. Fernando. My mother. Several messages from the foundation. A reporter from the Times of London. Another from the BBC. A friend in New Hampshire offering condolences. Jenn Donnarumma, the liaison in the prosecutor's office, telling me that the defense had rested, the jury had gone into session, the verdict could come at any time, please hurry if you can.

A WhatsApp message caught my eye—from Daniel Rye Otteson, the young Danish man who shared a cell with Jim years ago, the one who had memorized the precious letter. He had to leave the trial and return to Denmark. *Sorry to miss you.* I called him immediately and he picked up on the first ring.

He, too, was in a taxi, on his way to the airport, travelling in the exact opposite direction to catch his flight back to Europe. In fact, the two taxis could have been passing each other somewhere on the highway that very moment: this was the modern world, with signals coming and going in all directions.

"It's so good of you to come all the way," I said.

He could not have done otherwise, he said. We were all a community, bound together. He felt the presence of Jim and the others in the courtroom. His testimony had been harrowing but it had gone well. (I found out later that Daniel talked about his capture and release, but he had also talked about how he had been tortured too, being hung from the ceiling by chains, beaten on his feet, starved. And he talked, too, graphically, about his own suicide attempt in his cell. I was relieved, for a moment, to have been spared those words and the idea of that sweet young man swinging from a bar in the light of a Syrian prison window.)

I knew that Daniel—like so many others—still carried the wounds behind the words. The guilt. The flashbacks. The fresh scars that nobody but the closest loved ones ever really saw. The sadness that probed through to the opposite side.

Still, the call brightened me, gave me solace and brought me back into the fold.

"Thank you, Daniel," I said. "Look after your beautiful family. God bless."

Upon hearing the blessing, my taxi driver—Samir, a Middle Eastern man—glanced in the rearview mirror and gave me a smile.

These small moments—they, too, were part of the latticework.

I closed my eyes, tried to sleep, but within minutes, it seemed, the cab pulled up outside the federal courthouse. I glanced at a small cluster of cameras set up on the outside lawn. Reporters and photographers were milling about. Some other bystanders. I wondered if I had time to go to the local church to pray for Rita, but it was a half-mile walk, and I didn't want to miss the verdict. Rumors abounded. Some were saying that the jury, staying late, had asked for a clarification, and an announcement was expected within moments. But another person said that there has been a problem of interpretation with the language on the jury docket, and it may now take days to get a verdict.

I set up in a coffee shop across from the courthouse and opened my phone once again. On the screen was a picture of Rita, sitting in a meadow of Texas bluebonnets, on another day, another time, far away. The time ticked as time does: five o'clock, six o'clock, six thirty.

In this place of waiting, Lord, help me remain faithful.

At six forty-five I looked up and saw a man in a security uniform sprinting across the lawn in front of the courthouse. Was there a decision, then? A verdict? An emergency?

I gathered my belongings and stepped quickly outside the café but knew immediately from the slump of the reporters' shoulders, the way the cameramen were bending to fold the legs of the tripods, the way the shorthand notebooks snapped shut.

A huge disappointment washed over me: there would no verdict tonight.

In the end there was no doubt. The jury came back early the next day. Guilty on all counts. There was no gasp in the courtroom. No outrage. Elsheikh hung his head. Sentencing was set, ironically, for August 19th, the anniversary of Jim's murder. But there was no doubt as to what the sentence would be: life imprisonment, a cell without a view, a time that stretched without reprieve.

Did I feel justified to see him found guilty? Of course I did. Elsheikh deserved to be sentenced as harshly as possible. But for me the moment was shot through with an ineffable sadness too. A life sentence. What is a life? What does it bring? What does it represent? The prospect of spending all but one hour of a day, every day, in a jail cell has never seemed to me to be a form of true justice. Did he need that much time to ponder the consequences of his actions? Maybe so. Did he need to be kept in a tiny room? Maybe so. Did he need to be monitored until the end of his days? Maybe so. But nothing was going to bring Jim back. My son was gone. The only solace was that Jim would never be forgotten. That's what mattered most to me. I knew in my heart that it was what would matter to every mother, the world over.

Elsheikh had a mother too. I had to acknowledge her heartbreak, far away, in London. I lowered my head and said a prayer for her.

He was led away by two officers of the court. He didn't even glance over his shoulder.

I suppose at a certain stage you have to bid goodbye to a portion of your life. For an instant you almost hover outside of yourself. You float in the air. You look down. You take stock of what you believe in. You see yourself clearly, or at least as clearly as you will allow yourself to see. I was 73 years old. It was eight years since my son had been killed. I had learned a great deal about my life and the world. I had seen enough sadness to fill every molecule around me. I had been forced to contemplate all the worst things that the world had to offer. I had been lonely, and I had been lost. I had been led to the edge of despair. But I had also seen some of the greater things that the world can reveal from behind the pain. I didn't need to succumb to the dark. I could feel God's presence in the good and earnest people around me.

I waited at the back of the courtroom. I hugged the other parents. Some of them were in tears. I could feel their bodies loosening. The ordeal was not over, but it had found the possibility of an ending. The back of the courtroom filled. I shook hands with the prosecutors. It was a victory for them. They saw it—and rightly so—as an illustration of justice. But I also shook hands with members of the defense team who had gathered at the back of the courtroom too. They had sat with Elsheikh for many months, and they had tried to argue for his freedom. It was part of their job and part of their dignity too. They believed in the wider world of justice.

One of the defense team came across and whispered to me that it was the most difficult thing she had ever done in her life. She wished she did not have to do what she had done. "I'm sorry," she said. But the truth was that she didn't need to be sorry. I respected her as much as I respected those who had helped put my son's murderers away. She had been true to the principles of her profession, but she had also been true to a deeply held belief in justice.

There is so much about America and our government that I have learned to question over the years—our assuredness, our isolation, our arrogance, our ability to turn justice into revenge—but this was the benevolent face of justice that I was encountering. This was America too. This was the complicated and purposeful truth. I hugged her. She, too, felt relief. I could feel it float from her.

Just over her shoulder, I saw Jenn Donnarumma from the prosecutorial team. For the past 18 months Jenn had helped put together virtually all the logistics for the trial. She had been in touch with every witness, every parent, every expert. She had liaised with the lawyers, booked all the flights, arranged the hotel rooms. She had created flow charts. She had molded the entire schedule. Jenn's whole life had been given over to the trial. There were times when she had worked eighteen-hour days and then arrived early to work the next day. She was hugging the other mothers and saying her goodbyes. She was, for the first time in a long time, about to take a holiday. She was in a little bit of a rush since her kids had already left a couple of days beforehand. They had gone on ahead with their father, and now they were waiting for her to finally join the family vacation. She was so happy. She couldn't wait to see her children. But she would keep her phone on, she said, in case anybody needed to contact her.

She walked briskly towards the elevators. Others were crowding in beside her. I squeezed my way in too. The round stickers advising us to remain several feet apart were still on the floor, slightly scuffed now from all the wear and tear.

I thought of all the pain the elevator had carried up and down over the previous couple of weeks. It was a world of opposites. Up and down. Good and evil. Claim and counter-claim. Prosecution and defense. Freedom and incarceration.

We took the elevator down.

We were going home.

We are always going home.

BOOK THREE
Don't Try the World Without Him

1

June 2022
Wolfeboro, NH—Alexandria, VA

The email comes through in the late afternoon. Three PDF letters from Alexanda Kotey. Sent by the prosecutor's office. Two of them addressed specifically to her.

She is at home with John, and they have guests—their son John Elliot and their grandson. She doesn't want to spend too long on her phone in front of her grandchild—simply for the sake of manners. What sort of grandmother does that? Still, she catches a brief glimpse of the files after they download. The largest document—on official paper—seems to contain Kotey's letter to the judge prior to his sentencing. The other two are handwritten. Addressed specifically to her. *Dear Mrs Foley.* The writing is extraordinarily neat and sharp. On lined paper. With a thin pen. In a meticulous hand. One letter is short. A page only. The other is longer. Four or five pages. It is difficult not to disappear for a while to read them thoroughly. She glances at the dates. One is quite recent. *8 May 2022.* But the other is older. *October 30, 2021.* Written shortly after her visit with him. She scans the first line. *It was a pleasure to have had the opportunity to have finally met you.*

She wonders why it took so long for the letter to get to her. Some bureaucracy perhaps. Some problem with the SAMs, the Special Administrative Measures, the rules around Kotey's sentencing.

A sharp inhale: anticipation, dread, doubt.

First, she must print out the documents. That is the task at hand. Then find the time to read them properly. To let them settle. To understand them. To read into the core of what they are saying. Perhaps they contain the full admission she has been waiting for? No, not *waiting for. Expecting.* Not that either. *Hoping for*, perhaps. Or perhaps not that either. Maybe they will amount to a rant or a dark manipulation of the truth. Maybe Kotey has just written them to twist the events in his favor, or to pull the wool over everyone's eyes, even his own.

She moves through the kitchen and into the adjacent living room. The printer whirrs and coughs. The largest file is 79 pages long. She allows it to print first. The noise of it rattles through her head. *United States of America vs. Alexanda Amon Kotey. Defendant's Position on Sentencing.* An argument, she presumes, for where he is to spend his days in prison. The sentencing is already determined but the prison itself is all-important. What Kotey wants to avoid is the Super Max prison in Colorado where he will be condemned to near-permanent solitary confinement.

On the screened-in porch she says nothing to her family: the generations of Foley men. Her husband and her son are well used to this—the ringing of her phone, the buzzing of texts, the sound of printing pages. They don't want to engage. At least not right now. It bothers her sometimes, but it's something that she must respect. The Jim they love is a Jim who lives in the past. They want him to remain there. To remember him as he was. She understands. They don't need to know or hear from or about Jim's killer. At least not yet. There is a part of her that feels the letter should be hers for a while anyway. She should keep it close. Fully inhabit it.

She rises from the porch and walks back through the kitchen, into the living room where the last page—or rather, the first page, written two days after meeting her last October—is printing out.

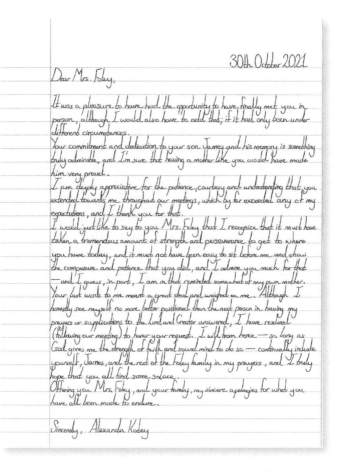

30th October 2021

Dear Mrs. Foley,

It was a pleasure to have had the opportunity to have finally met you in person, although I would also have to add that; if it had only been under different circumstances.

Your commitment and dedication to your son James and his memory is something truly admirable, and I'm sure that having a mother like you would have made him very proud.

I am deeply appreciative for the patience, courtesy and understanding that you extended towards me throughout our meetings, which by far exceeded any of my expectations, and I thank you for that.

I would just like to say to you Mrs. Foley that I recognize that it must have taken a tremendous amount of strength and perseverance to get to where you have today, and it must not have been easy to sit before me and show the composure and patience that you did, and I admire you much for that — and I guess, in part, I am in that reminded somewhat of my own mother.

Your last words to me meant a great deal and weighed on me. Although I honestly see myself no more better positioned than the next person in having my prayers or supplications to the Lord and Creator answered, I have resolved (following our meeting) to honor your request. I will from hence — so long as God gives me the strength of faith and sound mind to do so — continually include yourself, James, and the rest of the Foley family in my prayers, and I truly hope that you all find some solace.

Offering you Mrs. Foley, and your family, my sincere apologies for what you have all been made to endure.

Sincerely, Alexanda Kotey

It startles her in many ways. The neatness of the handwriting. The politeness. The courtesy. The construction of the sentences. Their careful articulation. *I was deeply appreciative.* The beseeching and respectful tone. The appeal to familiarity. *Reminded somewhat of my own mother.* And the final words. *Offering you Mrs Foley, and your family, my sincere apologies for what you have been made to endure.* She stands over the printer and closes her eyes. She is not quite sure what yet to feel about the tangle of words. Is it God's grace? Is it a proper reckoning with truth? She wishes that she had the original letter and that it had come through the post box months ago, to hold, to weigh, to ponder. But this is so much of her life now: it is digital, and the original note is held in the hands of others. It is an apology, yes, and a deeper one than when she spoke with him in October. Of course, there is always the tinge of doubt, but it rings of the real, although it still has an edge of equivocation. *For what you have been made to endure.*

She places the copy of the letter on the dining room table for anyone to see and then she walks back out to the porch where she ruffles her ten-year-old grandson's hair. She is happy to see him so content. There is a complicated world in front of him. Enjoy it now, she thinks. Embrace it. Revel in its simplicity.

Sometimes her own life now feels as if she operates on several different sets of moving swings, all of them independent and yet also interlaced. There hardly seems like a free moment in any day. So much to do. So many things to catch up on.

But, oh, that letter. It has pierced her. She wants to return to it and read it again. But give it time, she tells herself.

Let it settle. It will always be there.

He showed her the photograph eight months ago. It burned a place in her memory. His three daughters. There was an air of the unreal about it. They wore pink and powder-blue dresses. Their hair was neatly pulled back. They were beautifully presented, their dark eyes, their sallow skin. They could have easily stepped from a recent catalogue.

They live, now, these girls, in a refugee camp in northern Syria. The conditions could hardly be worse. The camps are tightly controlled by militia forces. The tents are flimsy and flap in the wind. Medicine is random. Water is scarce. Food is too. Often, after the rains, the women have to wade waist-deep through the mud. The children have no access to schools. There are rumors of nearby rape camps.

In all these months she has not been able to shake the photograph from her mind.

She reads the second letter in its entirety at one-sitting, early that evening. *Dear Mrs Foley, I hope that you are well and that this letter finds you and your family while you are all in good health and the best state of well-being. Mrs Foley, during the meetings that we shared you may recall and have sensed my slight apprehension in comfortably expressing my explicit remorse and apologies. That was not due to the absence of those feelings and sentiments, but rather that they were intertwined and tangled with other emotions.* Such a formality of language. The tone is, dare she say it, elegant.

She reads on: *I would like to honor your intellect, patience and capacity for understanding by being entirely honest with you on how mixed I initially was towards your family. I can recall exactly how I felt back in 2016/17 while still inside the Islamic state as I sat alone and with no shame, I tell you, I wept watching 'The James Foley Story.' I was instinctively moved by compassion and sympathy for your collective anguish and grief as a family, whilst also feeling a sense of guilt for my role in what was inflicted.* A strong shiver of cold along her spine. She recognizes that word *whilst*. From the ransom e-mails. It was always a word that stood out. She takes a breath. Closes her eyes. She cannot forget that this is the same man who demanded money for her son's life. The same man who wrote Jim's last dying words. The same man who has pleaded guilty to conspiracy to murder.

She scrolls down through the letter. *However, I also found those feelings and sentiments being challenged by how I felt in regards to James' brother John's role as a U.S. military pilot. I had considered highlighting this in our meetings that was shared but then decided against doing so out of consideration for the subject's potential sensitivity for you personally, Mrs Foley, and whilst also acknowledging within myself that it was, at the time, an issue that perhaps I had not yet reconciled with.* A nick of doubt lances her. So, Kotey still thinks that James' brother, John—the same John Elliot whose voice she can now hear from the far side of the house—was a pilot! As if he had somehow dropped bombs from above! As if he was somehow culpable! He was in the U.S. Air Force, yes, but she feels the overwhelming sense that Kotey is trying to compare his actions with those of her third-born son. Absurd. And wrong. No, she thinks, there is no equivalence here, no, none at all.

Jim went to Syria to help the Syrian people. He wasn't there to plunder. Nor colonize. He was there to get to the core of the truth. He wanted to give others a front row view of the terrors of war. There can be no justification for what was done to him. No deflection of blame. None. Try the world without him. See what happens.

The letter seems to anticipate her doubt: *As I convey these words I seek your pardon if you find anything in them imposing, and I ask of you only that you once again kindly grant me that same patience you so gracefully extended to me throughout our meetings together. I would also like for you and your family to know that I write to you with the best intentions towards you all, in my humble attempt to clear some of the air. Having held in my own two hands the limbs and dead bodies of noncombatant men, women, and children (amongst them friends and loved ones) whom had perished in US airstrikes I had initially struggled to detangle—what can fairly be described as—those actions that had stoked our anger and those of our own misguided and unjust responses towards these grievances. Now far removed from all the clamor and commotion of war, some of my own afterthoughts on what transpired has allowed me to see things with a greater clarity.*

The letter continues in its high, formal style, quoting the Quran to say he was heedless to the injunctions of his faith, and he failed to observe proper justice. He addresses her son John directly: *I say to you, John: We do what we do in conflict and war.* He goes on to confess that, against the injunction of Islam, he must acknowledge that he did not spare the innocent in the way that he should have, and he further writes: *I am sincerely sorry to you for that.* She can only imagine the response of John Elliot, the fury that this half, or three-quarter, apology might invoke. *We did not observe justice when we discriminately burdened your family, and those of the other captives, with the sins of the U.S. government. Nor did we observe justice when subjecting you to all the graphic footage of the killings of your loved ones. I could go on with the injustices and inequities committed, and for what they inflicted of anguish, grief and sorrow I can only offer my sincere regrets and apologies.*

The letter ends: *Mrs Foley, to you and all of your family; my sincere apologies, regards, and best wishes to you all. Sincerely, Alexanda Kotey.*

She has to hold her breath when she finishes. What to feel about all this? How to acknowledge her confusion? How to feel about the depth of Kotey's soul-searching? Is it truthful? Is it just a patching up of his soul? Is he fooling himself? Is it just a well-constructed dodge? Is he just forgiving himself with an artful ease?

Within her own family there will, she knows, be several schools of thought. The first school is primarily her own: a gratitude, at last, for an apology that seems to genuinely come from the heart. The second school, those of John and John Elliot: a fierce anger that she might even read the letters or be in touch with Kotey at all. The third school: a combination of these two. And the fourth, the school of the future, her grandchildren: who is to tell what they and their cousins will think?

Soon—very soon—Kotey will be sent off to prison. He will be put in solitary confinement and remain there for the rest of his life. The plea agreement, where the victims and their families can talk to him, will become something that she will be unable to do.

If she wants to talk to him—her son's killer—again, there is one last chance.

Should I go? Should I not? Surely all of this is finished now? Surely there is no point in seeing him again?

She glimpses her grandson, outside on the front lawn,

about to catch a ball in mid-air. She places the letter on the table, closes her eyes for prayer.

———————————————

She is an American mother. It is not a story that often gets told. Hers is a small sky though it contains so much rain. The story sometimes forgets her. She is often invisible. She dissolves at the edge of someone else's words. But she has decided, quite against the grain, that the world is available to her too. She has her place in it. She has something to say. She doesn't need to retreat. She is not a person to quiver and fade. She has learned to speak out, not loud and shrill, not thumping and masculine, but with politeness, respect, resolve. She has her belief in God. And her patriotism. And she has her belief in her family too.

She also knows that she has been lied to, at all angles, in so many places. She has been taken for granted. She has been patronized. She has been condescended to. She knows the world in many shades: as a child, as a woman, as a mother. But she is not here for silence. She must say what she feels.

There is a wrongness in the world, and she has to stand up to it in whatever small way she can. Even if it doesn't work. Sometimes you just know the right thing. Sometimes you just follow your instinct. If you do nothing, nothing gets done. She is prepared to risk herself. Risk embarrassment. Risk ridicule.

There is a song she heard recently while driving to the supermarket. She had to pull off to the side of the road to hear it properly. *There's a crack, a crack in everything, that's how the light gets through.* Such an ordinary moment, but it seems to her to be a proper truth. Somehow it all relates to the other men and women who are out there now, in other parts of the world, in their cramped cells, hostage to the dark.

A crack, the singer sang, in everything.

He sits with his hands folded in front of him. He wears a green jumpsuit with a white undershirt. His feet are shackled. His soft shoes are black, without laces, just straps. All the accouterments of incarceration. His beard has grown slightly longer since she saw him, but he has trimmed around the mouth and chin so that it doesn't seem quite so full. There is a paperback copy of Phil Klay's *Uncertain Ground* on the table in front of him, and a cardboard file of his papers, including, no doubt, the photos of his three girls. A coffee cup. A brown sandwich bag. He has put on muscle and looks even more broad-shouldered than before.

She cannot help it, but there is a little shiver of resentment as she steps across the room to take her place at the desk to the side of him: he is healthy and he is alive and he is being treated with the utmost of care. And yet she is glad, too, that he is being treated this way. To hold these contradictory ideas is the essence of the moment. Perhaps it is the essence of *every* moment.

"Good morning," he says, sitting upright.

"Good morning, Alexanda."

She settles in the seat six feet away from him. There is, of course, no handshake, no approach. If anything, there is an air of slight confusion because she is still unsure that she should be here at all. The letters had pierced her. She was grateful for them. Perhaps they were enough. She could have just put them in a drawer and locked it with a key, allowed the words to sit in their own darkness. Still, she was intrigued by his apology. His mind worked in curious ways. The formality of the language was stunning. So too were the sharp edges of the handwriting. She had wondered what might happen if she had it analyzed. It was nearly impossible to reconcile with the man who committed the horrendous crimes she had heard about during the Elsheikh trial. Kotey was an enigma. How was it possible to have two such different men within one man? Or perhaps that was what all men—and women—were? A pull-together of surprises. A collision of mystery. So much more than one thing. He was not just a Muslim. He was not just a Brit. He was not just a terrorist. He was not just a prisoner. He was nothing simple at all. He was polite. He was manipulative. He was smart. He was forceful. A person, like all people, of multitudes.

"Thank you for your letters," she says.

"You are most welcome."

"They came a little late. I don't really know what happened, Alexanda. The one you wrote back in October. I only got it a couple of weeks ago."

"I'm sorry to hear that."

"I was grateful for them. They meant a lot."

He nods, says nothing, takes a sip from his paper coffee cup.

"How are you doing, Alexanda?"

It is a trick she often uses: the repeated use of a name to alert the listener of her interest. Or maybe not so much a trick, as an acknowledgment. *I see you. I recognize you. I will listen. I will remember.* She does it with taxi drivers, with friends, with waiters, with just about everyone she comes across. And when she does it, people sit up differently, listen differently, react differently.

"I'm doing well, thank you," he says.

He smiles, looks away, glances back and then bridges his hands together. There are seven people in the room—one defense lawyer, two prosecutors and some officials from the FBI. Kotey wonders aloud where her family friend is, the one who originally accompanied her during the October visits. When she explains that his own lawyer objected to the presence of this friend, Kotey baulks. He asks for a consultation with his lawyer, and after a few moments the family friend—who has been waiting in a nearby office—is allowed to come in and sit beside her, to listen without interfering, without taking notes.

Diane takes a deep breath. She waits for Kotey to say something, but he is either polite or disciplined, or both at once.

"And how is your family, Alexanda?" she asks.

She is astounded to learn that his wife and children have managed to leave the refugee camp in northern Syria. They have made it into Turkey, he says. The children are studying English. He has written them letters and he has also been able to talk to his family in a supervised phone call. A quick flash across her mind: the girls in their pastel dresses. She asks the children's names, and he stumbles a moment, caught off-guard, then joltingly recalls them.

"I'm glad to hear that," she says. "I've been praying for them. If there is ever anything I can do to help, I would try to do so."

She does not tell him, but she has been reading about

the refugee camps and has been in touch with foreign correspondents, including the British writer Christina Lamb, another activist who has made a clarion call for women's rights. Diane has even contemplated trying to be in touch with the mother, Kotey's wife, to write a letter, or to make a phone call. Perhaps the children might need a little financial help? Or some assistance in their attempts to get visas? It is not something she has acted on, nor even told anyone about, not even John, but it hangs there on a thread in the back of her mind. The children, after all, were collateral damage. Why should they suffer for what their father has done? Why should they not have a chance in the world? It would be a simple thing to do, surely. Just to show some concern. To widen the world. To extend the forgiveness into another space.

"You've had a lot of time to think," she says. "Do you have anything you want to ask me?"

"No," he replies.

It doesn't surprise her that he chooses not to return the favor. He is not interested in her or her family. He is a man in his own world. So many men are. It is not something to dwell on. She is confident enough. But it saddens her, at her core. The three girls. And yet what can she do? If the opportunity comes, she will help. It is what Jim would have done. That alone is enough.

For a moment their talk is stilted, jolting, polite. They edge around the letters. She invokes a scripture from the Quran that he has quoted: *Never let hatred of anyone lead you into the sin of deviating from justice.* He says that it was never a question of hatred for him, but he had done what he thought was right. It was true that he had, he says, put aside certain things of his faith and he had explained that in his letters. She has read in a letter that he sent to the judge that "our lives were simply humming along to the drumbeat of war." It was his way of explaining himself. He developed a layer of numbness, he said. "It could be asked if we lost some of our humanity? I would have to say with all honesty that I could not decisively answer that question with such simplicity." She is fully aware that he still feels that he did what he did in the fog of war. He still does not find himself fully culpable. His were the actions of a soldier. Sometimes misguided and sometimes misdirected, but always, in his opinion, within the confines of war. He mentions Donald Rumsfeld and "enhanced interrogations" and the manner in which language was adapted to justify torture in Abu Ghraib. She understands it. She gets it. She might even agree with it. But that doesn't mean that she has to like it. She increasingly can see that he's a man who has perfected his equivocation.

He says that he is hopeful now. He is glad to have these meetings. It is important to understand one another, he says. He is still a realist, but he finds the meetings to be a silver lining. *A silver lining*, she thinks. It is not anything near what she is searching for. But if it is, for him, a silver lining, then let it be.

"I still have some questions, Alexanda. Some things about Jim. And about you."

"Please," he says.

"In all that time, have you changed your mind about anything?"

"Most of what I changed my mind about I put in the letters. I am better at saying what I want to say in letters. It gives me time to contemplate what I really want to say."

"Anything you thought about Jim?"

"Not that I haven't already said. Like I said, I thought he was straightforward. When I first met him I thought he was being sarcastic about his faith. But he wasn't. They were naïve questions. Like I said before, he was an optimist. How should I say it? A simpleton."

"A simpleton? Jim was the furthest from that."

"I don't mean that in the way you think. Not in the way you understand it. I mean it as a compliment."

"A compliment?"

He is good with language. But not this. *A simpleton?* She finds herself on high alert. A part of her reaches inside herself to understand. Perhaps he wants to talk about simplicity of thought, of clarity, of honesty? But it riles her. A word has been pushed under her skin. She does not like the conflagration of optimism with simplicity. It seems, in itself, naïve. Cynics are so often that way. So assured of themselves. It is their own form of sentimentality.

"Do you think you were brainwashed under ISIS?" The directness startles him for a moment. He extends his feet under the table and the shackles tighten.

"No." She knows that he needs time to think, that he needs to unravel. He takes the moment and seizes it. She allows it because she needs to collect her own thoughts.

There were many reasons why he got involved, he says. He had become Muslim at a young age. He questioned his lifestyle. "All the flashy stuff in Notting Hill." But he wasn't really a true believer. It took a while for his true faith to take hold. By the time he went to Syria, however, he had already lost some friends and he had found a humility within Islam. He was influenced by the Salafi school of thought and the jihadists that he met returning from the battlefields of Afghanistan. He found there a genuine bond of brotherhood and a clarity of belief, and he began to see that there was an unjust assault on Muslims all over the world. When he arrived in Syria he immediately launched into the fighting. By the third day he had his first major military operation. It was his first time to hold an assault rifle.

"Is there anything that you regret?"

For an instant his eyes roll slightly higher in his head. It is as if a lurking violence has rolled through him, and he must contain it. But it is there. For sure. It is there.

"I don't regret going, but I do regret some of the things that I did. There are times I wish I did not do the things that I was ordered to do. I wish I could have stopped myself. But that is hindsight. When you're in the thick of war you don't have an opportunity to pause and reflect."

"Do you still maintain that you only hit Jim twice?"

"I have no reason to lie to you," he says.

She is well aware that there are many reasons for him to lie, not least to save face. He says to her that he has also had a recent chance to talk directly with Daniel Rye Otteson and they were able to talk to one another. They had discussed some of the beatings that Daniel had received, especially the "dead-leg" technique with which he tortured the Danish man. He is asked then about other torture techniques. He shakes his head as if he knows nothing. He glances at his lawyer when asked if he was ever present at a waterboarding, but then he shakes his head and says no.

"It's tragic," she says. "The whole cycle of violence, it's just tragic."

He knots his hands and stares down. He takes a long breath. He has, he says, maintained a "moral compass." The phrase disturbs her, but she says nothing. She watches him as he shifts again in his seat: he is a man who sometimes seems to want to get away from himself.

"I remember the one time," he says, "when we had James in a headlock. And I was involved. And he looked up at me. His facial reaction, I mean. The injustice of it. That was on his face. And I can't forget that."

He begins to tear up. Not like he did the first time, eight months ago, but he drops his head and seems to cry quietly. She wonders about the theater of it. The room feels like it is held in aspic. She will contemplate later if he has cried for what he had done to Jim, if he was truly sorry, or if he was crying for himself. Who, then, did the injustice belong to? For whom was the show of remorse? She has heard him talk of an eye for an eye. It was part of his justification. She has also heard him say that he, too, received terrible beatings at the hands of the Kurds after he was captured. Was that, then, an eye for an eye? And what did it mean? He has made an argument, too, against permanent incarceration. When she asks him what sentence he would give himself, he ducks away from the answer and starts talking about Islamic injunctions, how thieves now have their hands surgically removed in certain African countries. She wonders what part of him—his head, his heart—he might surgically remove for the sin of killing her son and the other hostages. But that, she realizes, is unfair of her to think. She agrees essentially with his prison sentence: life. He took the lives of others, after all. But does that justify, then, his eye for an eye? Ah, but it's complicated. It's all so complicated. The world is murky. That, too, is part of what makes it turn. Perhaps the energy of the world comes from doubt. Not knowing. The only certainty, for her, is God.

The question of forgiveness is a tension in the room. Diane allows a silence. It has, in itself, its own hum.

"A lot of people in western culture expect that people can ask for forgiveness and then it's just given," says Kotey. "But ultimately my God does forgive. He will forgive me. That's what I believe."

His answer sends another small shiver of resentment to the base of her neck. She, once again, understands his answer. In so many ways she aligns herself with him. But his answer has to be honest. It has to be true. And she is not sure if his answer is one of absolute, deep honesty. There is something distant in the way that he says it. Something aloof. *My God does forgive.* He is so convinced of himself. So sure of his own correctness. Perhaps this is what drove him to war. But perhaps we are all this way? Perhaps she, too, is rife with the exact same amount of certainty: too much.

She moves herself slightly in the seat. Silently she whispers a prayer. *Give me strength, Lord. Allow me compassion.*

He takes another small sip of his coffee.

Oh, it was a mistake. Surely it was. Oh. To come here. This time around.

The first time around she learned so much. She was able to tell him about Jim. She was able to knock him off his comfortable balance. Now he is practiced. Assured of his answers. He has carved out his own sense of admission and non-admission. There is an emptiness in his expression that surely comes from not entertaining any doubts about himself.

What am I doing here? What is it that I came for?

She always remembers how astounding it was to put the videotape in the recording machine and to watch the credits roll. There were clips on the internet, but it was difficult to find the extended recordings. Here, with the video, on the large screen, they could watch it all unfurl. As if in real time. As if they were actually there.

Marquette University. In the forum. He stood at the podium. He wore a brown jacket and blue-gray shirt. His hair was slightly longer than usual. He looked at ease. He was introduced to a round of applause.

"Thank you for the introduction," he said. "It was generous. Overly generous."

He smiled. The room hummed. "I'm not a hero. I'm not noble. I was just trying to do my work and I got in a bit of trouble."

It was shortly after he had returned from Libya. After being captured for the first time. It was, he said, the biggest mistake of his life to go to the front line that day. And now he was haunted by the death of Anton. They had to leave his body behind. It was one of the things that still rattled him. He wished that they could find the body.

When he came home, he said, he learned just how much people had cared. It humbled him. He wanted to repay his thanks to everyone. He wasn't sure if he ever could. He had worried about his career being over. But it was proper journalism. It was important. It would live on. That's what journalism was about: the truth. If you didn't tell the truth, then what would happen to the truth? What would happen to the families behind the front line? But it wasn't worth his life, he said. No matter what romantic inclination you have, no matter what ethic you think you have, it's never worth your life.

If she could have paused the tape there, she would have. What was his life worth? Apart from everything?

She could tell, as the tape unfurled, that there was something more behind those words. He was staring out at the camera, but he could have been looking beyond it too. He was present and elsewhere at the same time.

He knew, in the end, that there were so many stories still to tell. He believed that the world was made of other people. He didn't want to be cliché about it, but the lure of the front line was like a siren song. He had faith, even if it was shredded sometimes. He prayed the rosary. He knew that's what his mother and grandmother would be praying. And he thought about the idea of not going back. He understood that it would be risky. But he had to do it.

"You know the thing is, there's physical courage, right?" he said towards the end of the tape. "For some reason I have physical courage. But really when you think about it that's nothing compared to moral courage. If I don't have the moral courage to challenge authority, to challenge the system, to write about things that are going to have maybe reprisals on my career, if I don't have that moral courage, we don't have journalism."

And then she watches him pause a moment to study the

microphone in his hand, take it down from his lips, let the words hang there: "So I just think we've got to make sure we have the moral courage."

There is not much time left. The few hours that she has had with him are dissolving now. She is disappointed. She was never quite sure what to expect. She is 73 years old now and he is 38. He will never again be half, or less than half her age. Time tightens the gaps. She hopes that someday he will come to a true realization of what he has done. He is close, so close. But he is not there.

"There's something I've been thinking about for a long time. With the other families."

"Yes?"

"Do you know where his body is buried? Jim's? And the others?"

"I want you to know that I have been open with everyone from the very beginning," Kotey says, leaning forward. "I wish I could tell. I wish I knew. But I told the prosecutors, I told everyone. I don't know. I honestly don't know. If I knew, I would tell you."

She believes him. And what use would it be anyway? It would bring a certain closure, of course, to her and all the families, but all the Jim she carries—his spirit, his courage, his caring—she carries with her anyway. He is out there, and he is everywhere. In the stories of other people.

She knows that it is time for her to leave this room. To move on. She has been aware of it for an hour now, or more. She has been hanging on, almost bored, waiting for a revelation.

But there is none to come. She knows that now.

All the revelation that is, has already been.

"This is the last time I will see you, Alexanda."

It saddens her to think that in a short while he will be transported away from here, taken by federal airplane to Colorado, where his true incarceration will begin. No more sessions with victims. No more investigations from the FBI. He will be alone with his thoughts for all but one hour a day. It is, she has heard, uniquely difficult, a sort of psychological terror. She has read about it. The experts claim that it is mentally debilitating. They say that it is as clinically distressing as physical torture. Even the outdoor recreation is in a tiny cage.

"Do you know what the future holds?"

"I hope eventually I get a chance to go back to Britain," he says. "To see my family there. I'll be incarcerated, but I hope to be close to them."

"I will pray for you. I hope that you find your place."

"I hope so too."

"We know that all things work together for good for those who love God," she says, quoting Romans 8:28, "to those who are called according to His purpose." She closes the small red notebook in front of her. "Thank God for your faith. Jim had his faith too. I hope that you will use it."

"I will. I want to read and write. I would like to become wise."

"You have great potential, Alexanda."

She wonders if that is the truth. He might use his time in prison to better himself. But he might also use it for detriment, especially if, and when, he gets out of solitary confinement. To stir up hatred. To encourage violence in others. But then again, there are the *then agains,* the *what ifs.* What if, what if, what if. It is so difficult to know what to think. Difficult to hold fast to any idea except that of God and His Mercy.

She is at the moment of scooting back her chair. She glances around the room. She is grateful for all the people who have been with her on the journey. She thinks, then, again, of the little girls.

"If there is anything I can do for them..."

He nods and tells her that it is very kind.

Diane is not sure if he means it or not.

"I am so sorry," she says as she rises from her chair. "Everyone lost here. All of us." She pushes the back of the chair. "I hope you are given peace, Alexanda."

He remains seated. She takes her small handbag and tucks it under her arm. She crosses the floor between them. It is then that the rest of the room is frozen. They have not touched each other once in all the meetings, Diane Foley and Alexanda Kotey. There has been no reason to. Nobody has approached him. He has had no human contact except for his guards. He wears shackles. Still, she should not be stepping towards him. For so many reasons. Not least the traditional Muslim injunction—which she has forgotten—in relation to Muslim men not touching a woman who is not permissible. Only a mother, or a wife, or a sister.

She, Diane, is not permissible.

But she steps across and reaches out her hand to him. Kotey pauses a moment. What travels across his mind? What memories? What fears? What allegiances?

He stands.

Slowly he reaches out and shakes her hand.

"Peace be with you," she says.

When she leaves the room, Kotey sits down slowly, a little stunned as if he has just flown into the windowpane of his life. Another silence has descended all around. He is asked what it meant to shake her hand. He nods and creases his hands together.

He has not intentionally touched the hand of a woman in a long time, he says—not since years ago when he touched the hand of his wife—and he suspects he never will touch the hand of a woman again.

And why, then, he is asked, did he take Diane's hand?

He ponders a moment and says: "She's like a mother to us all."

———————————

Within a quarter of an hour she is out of the building and scrolling through her phone to order an Uber to take her into Washington, D.C. She has a meeting with a U.S. congressman who has supported the provisions of the bill that she has built to help other hostages. She will meet with him to ask for his ongoing support.

She rolls a red suitcase out in front of her. It has a small picture of Jim in plastic casing tied to the handle. Also, a sticker of him in silhouette: *James Foley, American Journalist.*

She waits by the side of the road for the car. The Uber is late, and the meeting is fast approaching. She checks her phone again. Across the street, at the hotel, she sees an idling taxi begin to roll in her direction. *Ah, good. Thank you, Lord.* She will, most likely, be on time. As if by design, the trunk flies open and she places the red suitcase in. She opens the taxi door and the first thing she does is to check the name of the driver.

"Hi, Elisabeth," she says.

Elisabeth is middle-aged, hefty, joyous, a jangle of bracelets around her wrist. A Gloria Gaynor song rolls out of the stereo. *I Will Survive.* Who is this woman and why is she driving a taxi? What has led her here? What's her story? What circumstances, what pains, what triumphs?

Diane notices a picture of two children hanging from the rearview mirror. It is indeed a world of mirrors: her children, my children, his children too. *We are watching,* they seem to say. *We are counting on you.*

"Beautiful kids," she says, as she adjusts herself into her seat belt.

"Thank you. Where are we going?"

"We're on our way to Congress, Elisabeth."

The car pulls slowly out into the light traffic. It's a twenty minute journey to the city, she knows. She leans back against the seat and for a moment closes her eyes. All her life, a long attempt to close her eyes and rest.

But she shook his hand. She made that gesture. And he received it.

Everything good, once begun, lasts.

Nothing ever truly ends.

Diane Foley

Colum McCann

Acknowledgements
Diane Foley

"You prepare a table before me in the presence of my enemies;
you anoint my head with oil; my cup overflows."

Psalm 23:5.

My heart overflows with deepest gratitude. I have experienced both the cruelest hatred of this world and its more powerful goodness and love. I thank God for loving me, encouraging me, forgiving me and granting me the following angels who have picked me up and given me hope.

Thank you to my steadfast, beloved husband John, to my cherished sons and daughters, Michael and Kristie, John, Mark, Brad and Katie, our seven precious grandchildren, to my ever-loving mother Olga, Rita, Fernando, Maria, Joseph, Martha and Bill, Bob and Paula, Bill and Sally, Meghan. Dan, Courtney, Kelly, Peter, Ryan, Will, Molly, Nick and their families for so generously helping build Jim's legacy of moral courage and for continuing it with their lives of goodness and commitment to others.

Thank you to faithful friends Beth and Gregg, Tim and Faith, Corrine and Bob, Renie and Larry, Mary and Ralph, David and Sheila, Bob and Maria, Charlie and Louise, Ginny, Nancy, work colleagues, generous neighbors like Walter and MaryEllen, devoted church friends like Jackie, MaryAnn and faith-filled servants of God: Father Marc Montminy, Father Paul Montminy, Father Robert Cole, Father Paul Gousse, Father Fred Zagone, and Sister MaryAnn Laughlin and Sister Mary Rose Reddy.

Our devoted Foley Foundation staff...Amy Coyne, Cindy Loertscher and Tom Durkin. Extraordinarily generous James W. Foley Legacy Foundation Board members, past and present: Doug Patteson, Gregg Roark, Jere VanDyk, David Rohde, Bill Ryan, David Levinson, Fernando Colina, Sarah Levinson Moriarty, Ellen Shearer, Tresha and Peter Bergen, Ali Soufan, Nick Rasmussen, Rana Altenberg, Jen Easterly, James O'Brien, Chris Costa, Peter Ventura, wise Foley advisors Mickey Bergman, David McGraw, Kathy Gest, Paul and Wendy Morigi, Joel Simon, Delphine Halgand, Margaux Ewen, Rachel Briggs, Liz Franks, Luke Hartig, Pat Rowan, Eric Lebson, Emily Lenzer, Mouaz Moustafa, Gary Noesner, Jason and Yegi Rezaian, Josh Geltzer, Rob Saale, Dana Shell Smith, Robert O'Brien, Sam Goodwin, Charlie Sennott, and Nizar Zakka.

Former strangers, now treasured friends, like David Bradley, Phil Balboni and David Rohde, who helped when others did not during Jim's captivity. The dedicated U.S. Department of Justice FBI agents, and stellar prosecuting attorneys and victims' advocates.

The hundreds of dear friends of Jim (FOJs) who rallied to help during his captivity and thereafter....Brian Oakes, director of *Jim, the James Foley Story*, Heather MacDonald, Bill Ryan, Michael and Kate Joyce, Tom and Barbara Durkin, Pat Durkin, Tim and Joana Mullen, Don Cipriani, Peter Pedraza, Daniel Presnell, April Goble, Rich Griffin, Daniel Johnson and so very many more generous colleagues from Marquette University, Medill/Northwestern University and University of Massachusetts. Thanks to brave journalist colleagues Nicole Tung, Claire Gillis, Manu Brabo, and Sean Langan.

Lastly, I am deeply grateful to the talented and

compassionate author Colum McCann for noticing a photo of Jim reading *Let the Great World Spin* and for helping me tell my story. Colum took a full year of his life to become a friend and accompany me to the trial and Kotey meetings. Thank you to his talented editor Bob Mooney, and Jim's dear friend Tom Durkin for patiently reading my edits.

Acknowledgements
Colum McCann

There are so many people to thank, not least Diane and John, and all of those who touched, and were touched by, and continue to be touched by, the life of Jim. A particular thanks to Allison and my family, my agent Sarah Chalfant, my assistant Max Krupnik and all at Etruscan Press, especially Phil Brady, Bob Mooney, Bill Schneider, Lisa Reynolds, Pamela Turchin and Amanda Rabaduex. Also, sincere thanks to Conor Mooney. Particular thanks to Gideon and all at the Moriah Fund. And, of course, to Lisa and all at Narrative 4.

Everyone, indeed, a story.

About the Authors

Colum McCann

Colum McCann, born and raised in Dublin, Ireland, has won multiple awards and honors for his seven novels and three collections of short stories. *Apeirogon*, his most recent novel, published in 2020, became an international best-seller on four continents. McCann serves as President and co-founder of Narrative 4, a non-profit storytelling organization which helps build empathy in young people, encouraging them to improve their communities.

Diane Foley

Diane Foley founded the James W. Foley Legacy Foundation to advocate for freedom for innocent Americans held hostage or wrongfully detained abroad, and for journalist safety. Foley has raised awareness about international hostage-taking through her government advocacy, the award-winning documentary, *Jim: the James Foley Story*, and opinion pieces in the *New York Times, Washington Post* and *USA Today*. She lives in New Hampshire with her husband, Dr. John W. Foley, and is the mother of four other children and seven grandchildren.

Etruscan Press extends heartfelt gratitude to the following patrons and their chosen honorees for supporting this title's publication:

Joseph Bednarik

Elizabeth Brack & Rob Kovell

Judy Garrett Brady

Barbara Brothers

Maeve Carpenter

Lisa Consiglio

Amy Coyne

Christine Curley

Gabrielle and Nick D'Amico

Theresa D'Angelo

Diane & Tom

Prof. Craig Duff

Andrea L. Edwards

Natalie Eilbert

Dennis M Fitzpatrick

Colin Flynn

Sandee G.

Guy Garcia

Ronald T Gauthier, Jr

Loretta Brennan Glucksman

Rusty Grace

Allison Hawke

Ashlee Harry

Heather

Ross Klavan

Susan Lawson

James Lennon

Joseph Lennon

Michael Lennon

Peter Lennon

Stephen Lennon

Lynn Lurie

Rob Mathes

Kristina Mooney

Maureen Mooney

Chris & Neda Morvillo

Faisal Mohyuddin &
Hina Sodha

In Memory of Dr.
Peter F. Mullany

The Oristaglio Family

In memory of Philip and
Jacqueline Pokrinchak

Julianne Popovec

Mary Poth

Rick Richards

Anne Reeves

Fran Skennion Reilly

Gideon Stein

Jessica Snyder

Mary Trinity

Michael Waters

Julie Sidoni Yelen

Books from Etruscan Press

Etruscan Press Is Proud of Support Received From

Wilkes University  Wilkes University

Ohio Arts Council

The Stephen & Jeryl Oristaglio Foundation

Community of Literary Magazines and Presses [clmp]

National Endowment for the Arts

NATIONAL
ENDOWMENT
FOR THE ARTS

Drs. Barbara Brothers & Gratia Murphy Endowment

Founded in 2001 with a generous grant from the Oristaglio Foundation, Etruscan Press is a nonprofit cooperative of poets and writers working to produce and promote books that nurture the dialogue among genres, achieve a distinctive voice, and reshape the literary and cultural histories of which we are a part.

Etruscan Press

www.etruscanpress.org
Etruscan Press books may be ordered from

Consortium Book Sales and Distribution
800.283.3572
www.cbsd.com

Etruscan Press is a 501(c)(3) nonprofit organization.
Contributions to Etruscan Press are tax deductible
as allowed under applicable law.
For more information, a prospectus,
or to order one of our titles,
contact us at books@etruscanpress.org.